BIGlittle
SCULPTURE

Library of Congress Cataloging-in-Publication Data

Tuchman, Phyllis.
   BIG little sculpture.

   1. Small sculpture, American—Exhibitions. 2. Small sculpture—20th century—
United States—Exhibitions. I. Williams College. Museum of Art. II. Title.
NB1277.T83   1988   730'.973'07401441   87-51597   ISBN 0-913697-04-4 (pbk.)

Williams College
Museum of Art
Main Street
Williamstown, MA
01267
telephone:
(413) 597-2429
telex:
5106018666

This Project is
supported in part by
a grant from the
National Endowment
for the Arts.
Organized by the
Williams College
Museum of Art with
the assistance of
funds from the New
England Foundation
for the Arts, a
private, nonprofit
organization which
develops and
promotes the arts of
the region. This is a
traveling exhibition
of the New England
Foundation for the
Arts.

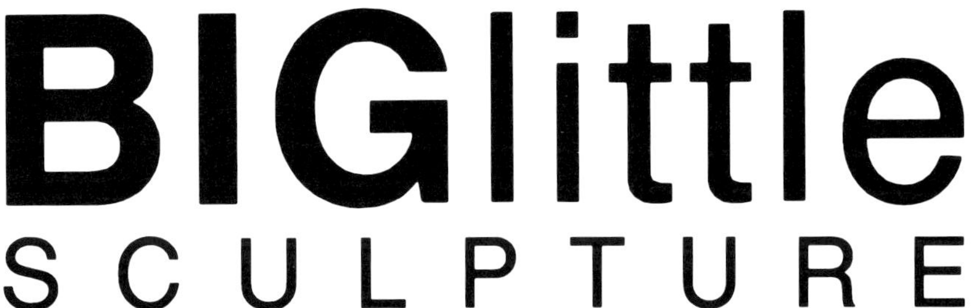

BIGlittle SCULPTURE

PHYLLIS TUCHMAN
Exhibition Curator

WILLIAMS COLLEGE MUSEUM OF ART

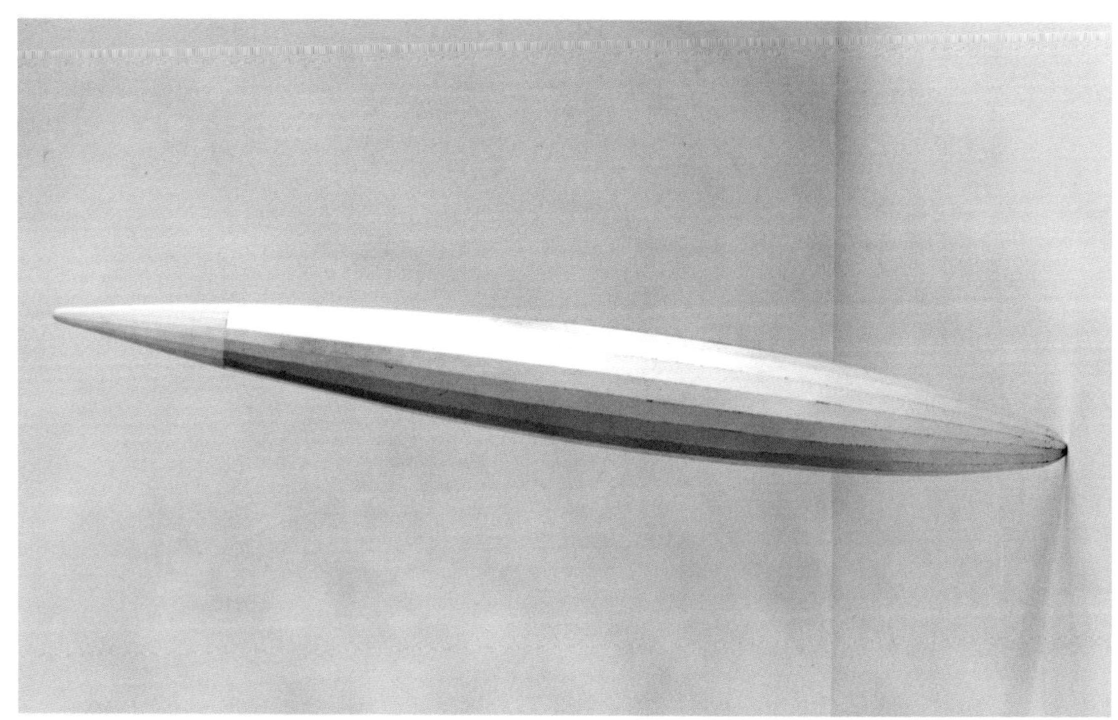

Bryan Hunt
King Crest, 1976
8 x 64 x 7 inches
Spruce wood, silk,
aluminum leaf
Solomon R.
Guggenheim Museum,
New York, Exxon
Corporation Purchase
Award
Photo: Robert E. Mates
and Mary Donlon

FOREWORD

Much of the sculpture of the last thirty years has been concerned with the issues of scale and material. As modernist attitudes in the early part of this century explored the intricacies and potential of shape, figure, and form in both representational and non-representational modes, scale and material per se were not singled out as issues of phenomenological investigation. Brancusi's *Endless Column* of 1934 was a beacon that heralded a new world of sculptural possibility, focusing on the physicality of the three-dimensional world that dominated advanced art well into the 1970s.

It is not without irony that Phyllis Tuchman has chosen a wonderful exhibition that at first glance would seem to challenge one of the basic attitudes of sculpture of the last few decades. Small-scale sculpture by large-scale artists reminds us in a delightfully understated manner of the pleasure of an intimate sculptural experience. Indeed the most extraordinary quality of this exhibition is the variety of concerns and issues that have been so powerfully addressed in works of modest scale. Ms. Tuchman shows us that good artists are multidimensional.

"BIG little SCULPTURE" was conceived and developed by Phyllis Tuchman, who also organized the exhibition, "Six in Bronze," at the Williams College Museum of Art in January 1984. A Visiting Lecturer in Art at Williams College in 1981-1983, she is the author of the respected Abbeville Press book on George Segal (1983) and an art critic for *New York Newsday*. The Williams College Museum of Art owes Ms. Tuchman a debt of gratitude for sharing this exhibition with us.

The staff of the Williams College Museum of Art assisted Ms. Tuchman throughout this project. Deborah Menaker, Associate Curator, and W. Rod Faulds, Assistant Director, oversaw and nurtured this show from the beginning. Mr. Faulds also lent his expertise to the design of the poster and catalogue. Vivian Patterson, Associate Curator of Collections Management, and Elizabeth Miller, Registrar, smoothly handled the registration and transfer of the objects to the museum. Saundra Goldman, N.E.A. intern at the Williams College Museum of Art, thoroughly researched the artists' biographies and bibliographies. Susan Dillmann offered her considerable editing and proofreading skills to the project. Mr. Faulds and Tim Ambrosino of Proforma in Pittsfield, Massachusetts designed a unique system of pedestals for the exhibition's installation which was implemented by George Abbott, Gary Sojkowski, and Tim Sedlock. Final thanks go to Sally Shafto, Assistant to the Director, without whose efforts these remarks would not have been written.

This exhibition was made possible through the generous support of the National Endowment for the Arts Museums Program and the New England Foundation for the Arts. The latter organization administered the tour of "BIG little SCULPTURE" at other venues through their Visual Arts Touring Program.

Thomas Krens, Director
Williams College Museum of Art

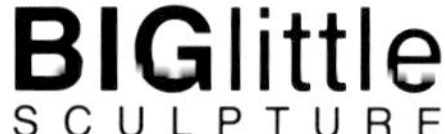

Sculpture once came in three sizes: small, large, and colossal. Gigantic religious and commemorative statues were commissioned for public places. Work in the five- to eight-foot range often was installed in church niches, in city squares and in front of civic buildings, or sited in private gardens. Forms that could be hand-held and collected by connoisseurs were frequently maquettes or models executed in fragile materials such as wax and clay.

Artists still make small sculptures. But these days they no longer create miniature or reductive versions of larger stuff, they conceive independent works. And when they scale their work unerringly, it seems monumental despite being measured with twelve-inch rulers rather than doubled yardsticks or engineer's chains.

Today's big little sculptures are different in other ways from comparably sized statues and constructions made during the distant and recent past. Avant-garde artists now model, carve, weld, and cast representational as well as abstract forms. They use all sorts of traditional and industrial materials that can be left in their raw state or colored. And they rest their pieces directly on the floor, against a wall, or atop specially designed pedestals or platforms.

Sculptors currently practice their craft in a more open-ended, less hidebound atmosphere. Consequently, big little sculptures are less uniform than the welded metal images and subsequent stark, geometric structures that prevailed for two decades following World War II. Although earthworks gained notoriety during the seventies and eighties, a greater number of form-makers executed small-sized work for various kinds of public and private spaces during this period.

Big little sculptures embody a host of new ideas and attitudes. Yet all sorts of debts and affinities to previous practices and themes may be discerned. By redefining the past rather than shunning its lessons, artists have invested their work with a timeless aura.

Modelled and cast figures by Willem de Kooning, Robert Graham, Clifford Ross, and Lucas Samaras could comfortably be included in a historical survey of bronze statuettes. As practicing modernists, however, each has extended the premises of traditional monoliths in fresh directions. Because viewers find surfaces that have been variously gouged and twisted in works by de Kooning and Samaras, they are more aware of the presence of the artist than they would be, for example, in front of a table-top form from the Renaissance. Ross's unique use of colored, three-dimensional backgrounds evokes powerful feelings about the settings for his naturalistic figures. Graham's women are remarkable in that they are ideal and realistic simultaneously. And by trying to tap, Graham says, the same kind of "resonance of emotions" the general public experiences during visits to monuments like the Lincoln Memorial, he calls attention to the belief that aesthetics are not always the sole criterion to be cited when evaluating sculpture or painting.

Ken Price's abstract ceramics also revise timeworn notions about art historical categories. Until recently his pieces would have been relegated to the decorative arts department of a museum. Because of artists like Price, who treat formal issues and develop subject matter in a manner that is as compelling as other big little sculptures, many fired and unfired clayworks are now installed amid the "high" art of their times.

Large, clunky minimalist objects and ephemeral, idea-oriented conceptual projects also have had an influential effect on the emergence of three-dimensional forms that can be hand-held. Joel Shapiro and Bryan Hunt amplified the implications of a style that hardly seemed adaptable to anything but a cumbersome size when they executed small sculptures with architectural subjects during the early and mid-seventies. They retained the sleek, spare look of minimalism as well as an interest in perceptual problems. They made the matter of size more meaningful to viewers, who know how large a house or an airship should be. Someone looking at one of their works can either feel like a behemoth or ponder the Twilight Zone-like notion that a nearby form must be far away in order to seem so small.

Beverly Pepper and Mel Kendrick have enhanced minimalist practices in other ways. The iron and steel sculptures Pepper forged and cast during the late seventies and early eighties are as bare, forthright, and object-like as any primary structure. However, rather than being baldly abstract, her works resemble ancient tools that have just been unearthed. Moreover, Pepper could not have ordered her art from a fabricator over the telephone because she carefully adjusted every edge and surface to her exacting specifications.

Kendrick's wood and bronze sculptures seem to have less in common with minimalism. But the artist has acknowledged the importance to him of Robert Morris's *Box with Sound of Its Own Making*, a sealed wood container housing a tape recorder that plays the noises made while it was being constructed. Without being didactic or ironic, Kendrick executes his work so that it also reveals the process by which it was formed. All the parts of each of his pieces come from a single block of material specifically selected for that sculpture.

Like Kendrick's art, work by Peter Gourfain and Tom Otterness hardly seems related to minimalism—or conceptualism. Yet the political orientation of their stylized figurative sculptures shares connections with the ethical and moral subtexts that were a part of many primary structures, dispersal pieces, and such. However, Gourfain and Otterness treat these themes overtly. Additionally, when Gourfain deals in apocalyptic reliefs with ecological issues, police brutality, and events in Chile, he links the present to the kind of horrific visions found on Romanesque church voussoirs that tourists mistakenly regard as no longer relevant to their lives. The black thoughts Otterness expresses in his reliefs and three-dimensional forms concern aspects of conformity and mechanization that he treats in a manner that recalls the art of the 1930s.

Joseph Cornell's boxes, the plaster foodstuffs Claes Oldenburg made for The Store in 1961, and the welded steel table pieces Anthony Caro initiated in 1966 can be cited as precedents for other big little sculptures. Like Cornell, Michael McMillen and Charles Simonds create miniature, uninhabited worlds that are eerily familiar and disconcerting. McMillen, a master of assemblage, uses all sorts of flotsam and jetsam to fashion ghost ships and the facades of abandoned buildings. The rubble-strewn cities and parched landscapes for "little people" that Simonds has convincingly rendered with unfired clay raise questions about global conditions and survival.

In her bronzes Nancy Graves has synthesized aspects of the seemingly irreconcilable: subject matter associated with Oldenburg's work and form language identified with David Smith and Caro. Instead of patinating or painting the casts of exotic blossoms, unusual foodstuffs, scissors, fans, and such that comprise a series of small welded sculptures she executed in 1983 and 1984, she baked enamel onto each element so that light shining on them fashions wondrous effects.

A history of welded metal sculpture has yet to be written, even though its practitioners have developed this style more fully and over a greater span of time than any other art form of the twentieth century. During the eighties Herbert Ferber, a member of the first wave of American artists to transform sheets and other units of steel, brass, lead, and the like into abstract shapes, used the bars of his signature cage to tether monochromatic canvas strips and metal ribbons to achieve work with the flavor of an elaborate pageant. Mark di Suvero, one of the few contemporary artists who has executed colossal structures, also has an uncanny knack for devising small sculptures with wonderfully inventive sections that turn and bob as they are touched by viewers.

Peter Reginato and James Wolfe belong to the latest generation of artists to weld metal sculpture. Like Ferber and di Suvero, they create their own unique shapes rather than relying on ready-made industrial components. Reginato's capacious works feel light and bouyant even though he makes his multi-hued organic forms from an intractable material. His art is open and airy because, like a master juggler, he has co-ordinated a complex number of parts. Wolfe packs his small brass sculptures with so many swooping curves and staccato-like struts that they call to mind ski slopes or amusement parks for lilliputians, types of imagery not ordinarily associated with formalism by its critics.

When one property such as size is kept constant in an exhibition like "BIG little SCULPTURE," new attitudes about other qualities are readily recognized. Sculptors active during the seventies and eighties certainly have not favored broad, generalized statements. They endow their forms and themes with detailed passages and specific data as if they were telling a story to a close friend rather than addressing a large, impersonal audience.

As the sixties have receded into the past, sculptors have rethought minimalist procedures. They use monochrome more sparingly. Many apply an abundance of color on the surface of their forms and their hues are hardly bland or standardized. The materials with which they work also reverse the minimalists' propensity for using unorthodox substances. Big little sculptures are executed from a wide range of materials that are also more traditional.

Many artists no longer consider pedestals, which were dispensed with during the sixties, as boxes upon which to prop their small pieces. They design the forms of their supports and calibrate their heights as meticulously as the works that rest on them. For example, Kendrick's stands occasionally look like his earlier work. And Samaras even casts the chairs on which he rests some of his figures.

Although big little sculptures that are representational and those that are abstract have shared a pool of practices, they differ in a few significant ways. The figurative forms usually have more stylized contours or surfaces that are less smooth and planar. They also tend to be smaller because their scale is as predicated on recognizable imagery as it was when artists executed maquettes for life-size statues. Geometric constructions, on the other hand, are larger because they incorporate greater pockets of space—breathing room for their many parts. Abstractions that have a monolithic character are either more compact or more elongated, and these aspects suggest that they, and the equally compact or elongated architectural sculptures, belong to opposite sides of the same coin.

When big little sculptures that are representational are juxtaposed with big little sculptures that are abstract, the seventies and eighties no longer seem like decades that can be characterized as being pluralistic. Too many connections between these two bodies of work exist for such a simplistic interpretation. "BIG little SCULPTURE" illuminates this period as one in which sculptors active in America radically integrated the traditions of the past with new dramatic attitudes about formal problems and life-affirming principles.

PHYLLIS TUCHMAN

ARTISTS

Willem de Kooning

Mark di Suvero

Herbert Ferber

Peter Gourfain

Robert Graham

Nancy Graves

Bryan Hunt

Mel Kendrick

Michael McMillen

Tom Otterness

Beverly Pepper

Ken Price

Peter Reginato

Clifford Ross

Lucas Samaras

Joel Shapiro

Charles Simonds

James Wolfe

Born: Rotterdam, 1904.
Attended Rotterdam Academy of Fine Arts and Techniques, 1916-1924.

SELECTED ONE-PERSON EXHIBITIONS

1953 Sidney Janis Gallery, New York. Also shows in 1956, 1959, 1962, and 1972.

1955 Martha Jackson Gallery, New York.

1967 M. Knoedler and Company, Inc., New York. Also shows in 1968, 1969, and 1972.

1968 Stedelijk Museum, Amsterdam. Traveled to Tate Gallery, London; The Museum of Modern Art, New York; Art Institute of Chicago; Los Angeles County Museum of Art. Organized by The Museum of Modern Art.

1969 XII Festival dei Due Mondi, Palazzo Ancaini, Spoleto.

1974 Walker Art Center, Minneapolis. Traveled to National Gallery of Canada, Ottawa; Phillips Collection, Washington, D.C.; Albright-Knox Art Gallery, Buffalo; The Museum of Fine Arts, Houston; Washington University Gallery of Art, Saint Louis.

1976 Stedelijk Museum, Amsterdam. Traveled to Wilhelm-Lehmbruck Museum der Stadt, Duisburg; Cabinet des Estampes, Musée d'Art et d'Histoire, Geneva; Musée de Peinture et de Sculpture de Grenoble.
Xavier Fourcade, New York. Also shows in 1979, 1982, 1983, 1984, and 1985.

1977 Museum of Contemporary Art, Belgrade. Organized by United States Information Agency and Hirshhorn Museum and Sculpture Garden, Smithsonian Institution, Washington, D.C. to travel to Eastern and Western Europe.
Fruit Market Gallery, Edinburgh, Scotland. Traveled to Serpentine Gallery, London. Organized by the Arts Council of Great Britain.

1978 Solomon R. Guggenheim Museum, New York.

1981 Guild Hall Museum, East Hampton.

1983 Stedelijk Museum, Amsterdam. Traveled to Louisiana Museum, Humelbaek, Denmark; Moderna Museet, Stockholm.
Whitney Museum of American Art, New York. Traveled to Centre Pompidou, Paris; Akademie der Kunst, West Berlin.

SELECTED BIBLIOGRAPHY

Ashton, Dore, and Willem de Kooning. *Willem de Kooning*. Northampton: Smith College Museum of Art, 1965.

Cummings, Paul, Joan Merkert, and Claire Stoullig. *Willem de Kooning: Drawings, Paintings, Sculpture*. Exhibition Catalogue. New York: Whitney Museum of American Art in association with Prestel-Verlag, Munich, and W. Norton and Co., 1983.

de Wilde, Edy, and Carter Ratcliff. *Willem de Kooning: Het Noordatlantisch Licht (The North Atlantic Light) 1960-1983*. Exhibition Catalogue. Amsterdam: Stedelijk Museum, 1983.

Forge, Andrew. *The Sculptures of de Kooning with Related Paintings, Drawings, and Lithos*. Exhibition Catalogue. Edinburgh, Scotland: Fruit Market Gallery, 1977.

Gaugh, Harry F. *Willem de Kooning*. New York: Abbeville Press, 1983.

Gohr, Von Sieghfor. *Willem de Kooning, Skulpturen*. Exhibition Catalogue. Cologne, West Germany: Kunsthalle, 1983.

Hess, Thomas B. *Willem de Kooning*. Exhibition Catalogue. New York: The Museum of Modern Art, 1968.

__________. *Willem de Kooning*. New York: G. Brazillier, 1959.

Larsen, Phillip, and Peter Schjeldahl. *De Kooning Drawings/Sculpture*. Exhibition Catalogue. Minneapolis: Walker Art Center, 1974.

Rosenberg, Harold. *De Kooning*. New York: Harry N. Abrams Inc., 1973.

Waldman, Diane. *Willem de Kooning in East Hampton*. Exhibition Catalogue. New York: Solomon R. Guggenheim Museum, 1978.

Willem de Kooning: Sculptures, Lithographies, Peintures. Exhibition Catalogue. Geneva: Musée d'Art et d'Histoire, Cabinet des Estampes, 1977.

Wolfe, Judith. *Willem de Kooning: Work from 1951-1981*. Exhibition Catalogue. East Hampton: Guild Hall, 1981.

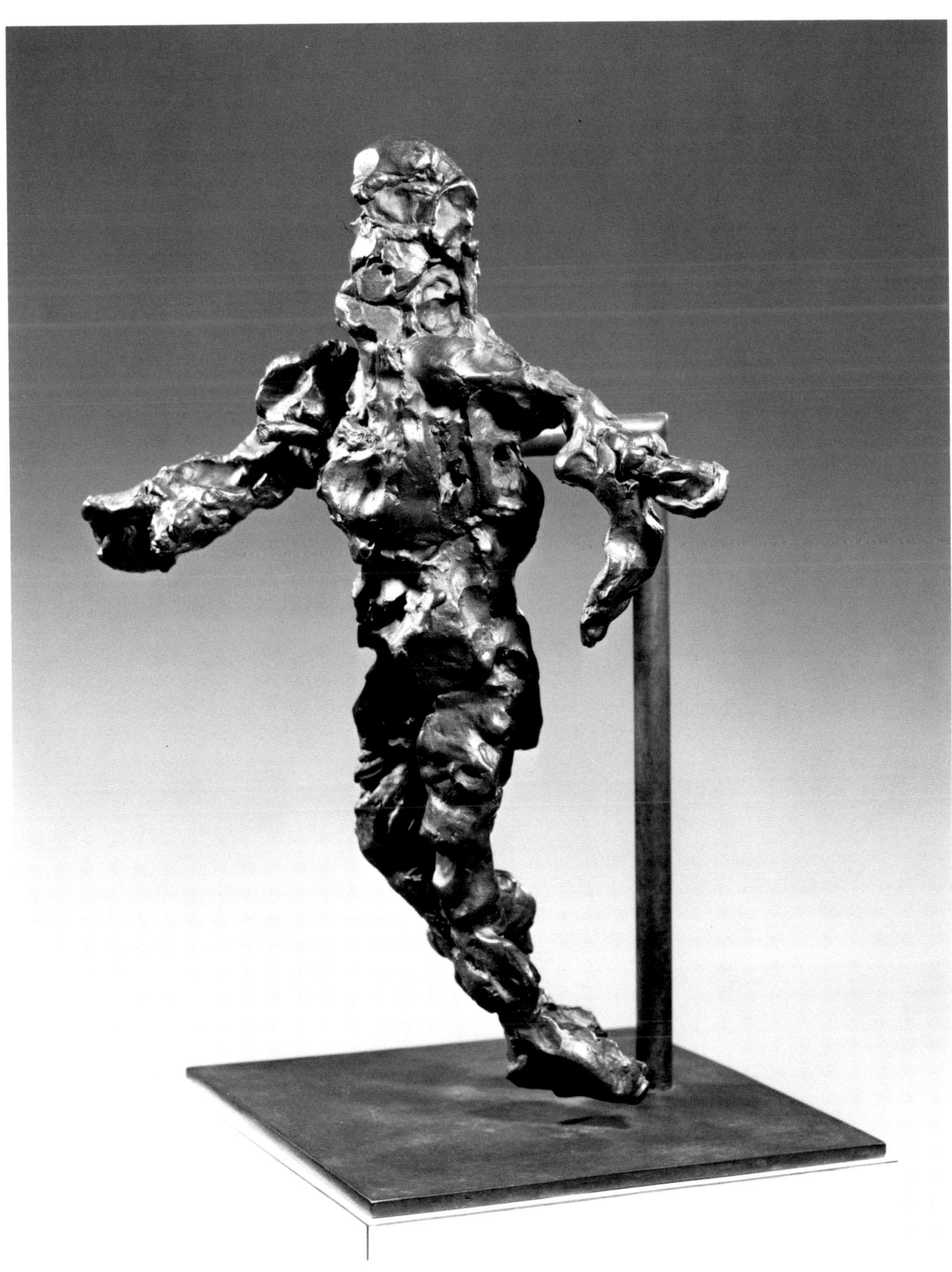

Untitled XIII, 1969
15¼ x 12¼ x 4½ inches
Bronze
David T. Owsley
Collection
Photo: Xavier Fourcade,
Inc.

MARK
di SUVERO

Born: Shanghai, 1933.
San Francisco City College, 1953-1954.
Studied at California School of Fine Arts and California Palace of the Legion of Honor, San Francisco.
B.A., University of California, 1956.

SELECTED ONE-PERSON EXHIBITIONS

1960 Green Gallery, New York.
1965 Dwan Gallery, Los Angeles.
1966 Park Place Gallery, New York. Also show in 1967.
1972 Stedelijk Van Abbe Museum, Eindhoven, The Netherlands.
Wilhelm-Lehmbruck Museum der Stadt, Duisburg, West Germany.
1975 Jardin des Tuileries, Paris.
Whitney Museum of American Art, New York.
1976 Hansen Fuller Gallery, San Francisco. Also shows in 1977 and 1979.
1983 Oil & Steel Gallery, New York and Hallets Cove, Long Island City. Also show in 1985.
1985 Storm King Art Center, Mountainville, New York.

SELECTED BIBLIOGRAPHY

Baker, Elizabeth C. "Mark di Suvero's Burgundian Season." *Art in America* (May-June 1974):59-63.

Evrard, Marcel, and Barbara Rose. *Mark di Suvero*. Exhibition Catalogue. France: Chalon-sur-France, 1975.

Geist, Sidney. "A New Sculptor: Mark di Suvero." *Arts Magazine* (December 1960):40-43.

Goddard, Donald. "Mark di Suvero: An Epic Reach." *ARTnews* (January 1976):28-31.

Hughes, Robert. "Energy as Delight." *Time* (December 1, 1975).

Kozloff, Max. "Mark di Suvero: Leviathan." *Artforum* (Summer 1967):41-46.

Kramer, Hilton. "A Playful Storm of New Sculpture." *New York Times Magazine* (January 25, 1976):10, 42-50.

Monte, James K. *Mark di Suvero*. Exhibition Catalogue. New York: Whitney Museum of American Art, 1975.

Ratcliff, Carter. "Mark di Suvero." *Artforum* (November 1972):34-42.

Rose, Barbara. *Mark di Suvero: New Sculpture*. Exhibition Catalogue. Houston: Janie C. Lee Gallery, 1978.

__________. "On Mark di Suvero: Sculpture Outside Walls." *Art Journal* (Winter 1975-1976):118-125.

Tuchman, Phyllis. *Mark di Suvero*. Exhibition Catalogue. Mountainville, New York: Storm King Art Center, 1985.

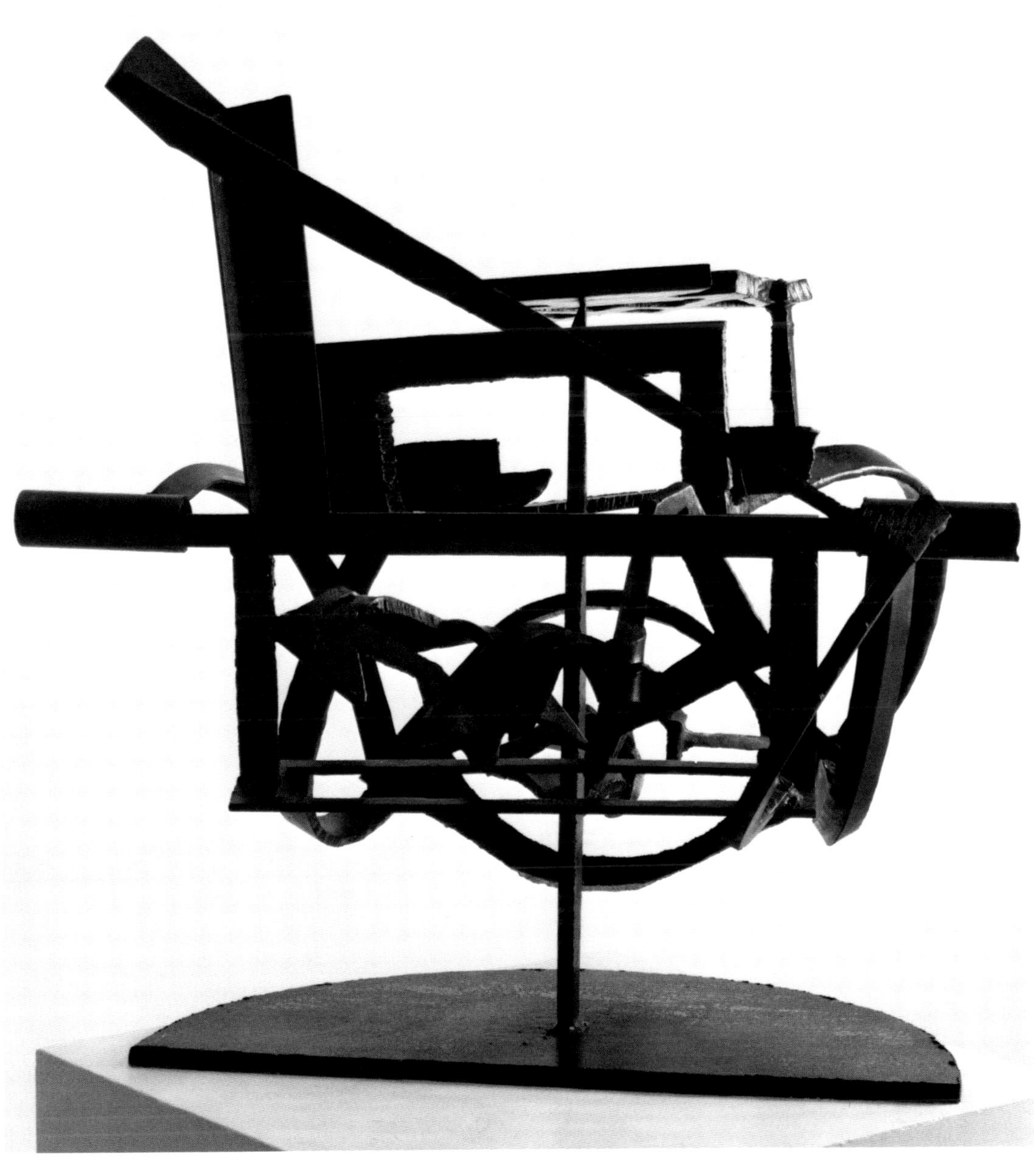

Search for Origins, 1983
32 x 29 x 40½ inches
Steel
Private Collection,
New York

HERBERT FERBER

Born: New York City, 1906.
College of the City of New York, 1923-1927.
B.S., Columbia University, New York, 1927.
Studied sculpture, Beaux Arts Institute of Design, New York, 1927-1930.

SELECTED ONE-PERSON EXHIBITIONS

1947 Betty Parsons Gallery, New York. Also shows in 1950 and 1953.
1957 Bennington College, Bennington, Vermont.
1960 Andre Emmerich Gallery, New York. Also shows in 1963, 1965, 1967, 1969, 1970, 1972, 1974, 1975, and 1977.
1962 Walker Art Center, Minneapolis. Traveled to Des Moines Art Center; San Francisco Museum of Art; Dallas Museum for Contemporary Arts; Santa Barbara Museum of Art; Whitney Museum of American Art, New York.
1978 M. Knoedler and Co., Inc., New York. Also shows in 1979, 1980, 1981, 1982, 1983, 1984, 1985, and 1986.
1981 The Museum of Fine Arts, Houston. Traveled to Des Moines Art Center.
1984 The Berkshire Museum, Pittsfield, Massachusetts.

SELECTED BIBLIOGRAPHY

Agee, William G. "Herbert Ferber: Painting, Sculpture, and Drawing, 1945-1983." *Arts Magazine* (April 1983):90-103.

______________. *Herbert Ferber: Sculpture, Painting, Drawing: 1945-1980*. Houston: The Museum of Fine Arts, 1983.

Balken, Debra Bricker, and Phyllis Tuchman. *Herbert Ferber: Sculpture and Drawings, 1932-1983*. Exhibition Catalogue. Pittsfield, Massachusetts. The Berkshire Museum, 1984.

Dennison, George. "Sculpture as Environment: The New Work of Herbert Ferber." *Arts* (May 1963):86-91.

Faison, S. Lane, Jr. "The Sculpture of Herbert Ferber." *College Art Journal* (Summer 1958):363-371.

Goldwater, Robert. *Herbert Ferber: First Retrospective Exhibition.* Exhibition Catalogue. Bennington, Vermont: Bennington College, 1957.

Goodnough, Robert. "Ferber Makes a Sculpture." *ARTnews* (November 1952):40-43, 66.

Goosen, E.C. *Herbert Ferber.* New York: Abbeville Press, 1981.

Rubin, William S. "Herbert Ferber's Sculpture in the Seventies." *Art International* (February/March 1976):28-33.

Tuchman, Phyllis. "An Interview with Herbert Ferber." *Artforum* (March 1971):52-57.

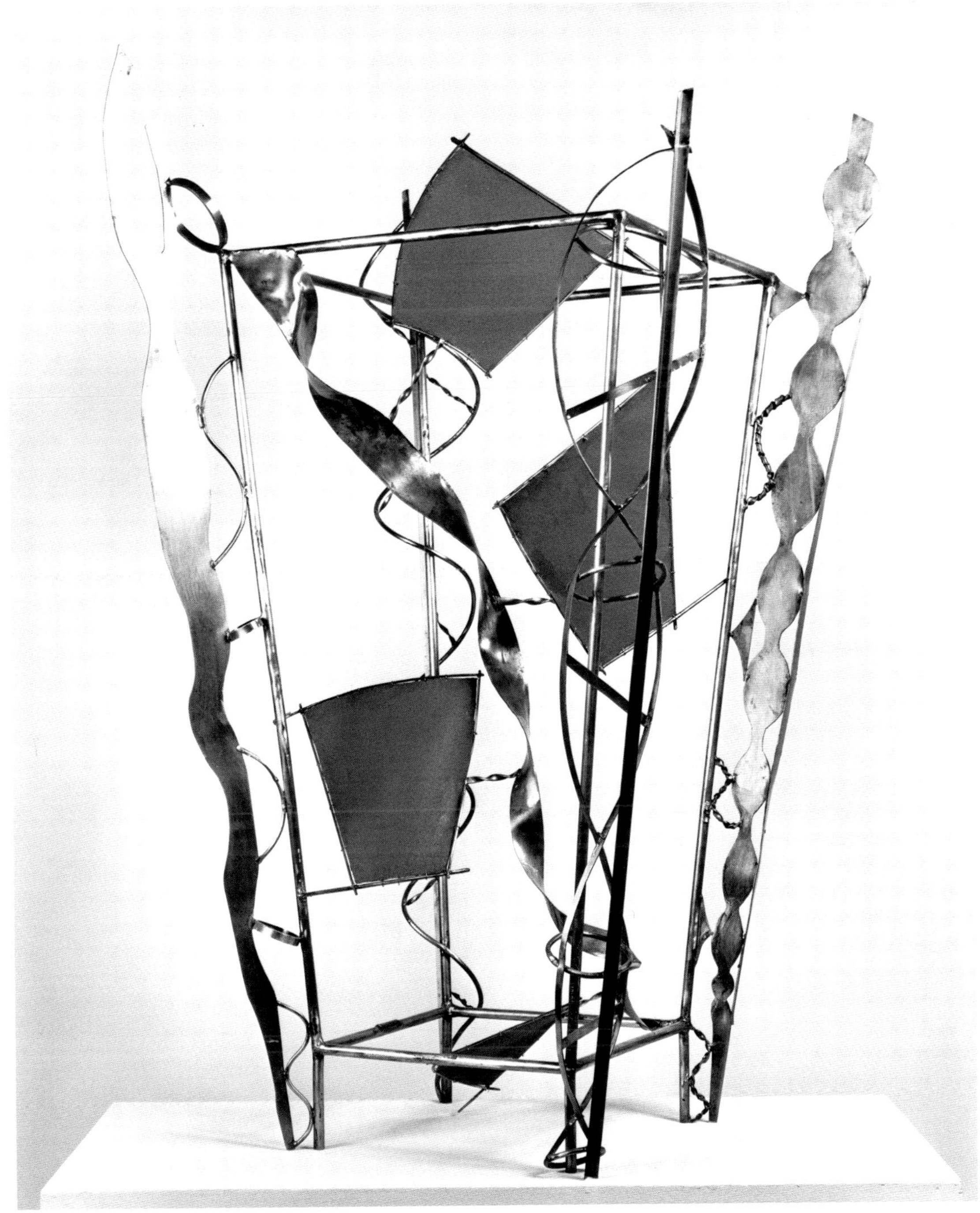

Semaphore Series #5,
1983
49 x 28 x 27 inches
Brass, copper, and
painted canvas
Collection of Edith
Ferber
Photo: Ken Cohen

PETER
GOURFAIN

Born: Chicago, 1934.
B.F.A., School of the Institute of Chicago, 1956.

SELECTED ONE-PERSON EXHIBITIONS

1967 Bykert Gallery, New York. Also shows in 1971, 1972, and 1973.
1982 Studio, Brooklyn. Six-year project with terra-cotta panels and carved wood columns.
1986 The Brooklyn Museum, New York.

SELECTED BIBLIOGRAPHY

Castle, Ted. "Peter Gourfain: Seafarer Plies His Troth." *Art in America* (May/June 1979):128-131.

Kotik, Charlotta. *Peter Gourfain: Roundabout and Other Works*. Exhibition Catalogue. Brooklyn: The Brooklyn Museum, 1987.

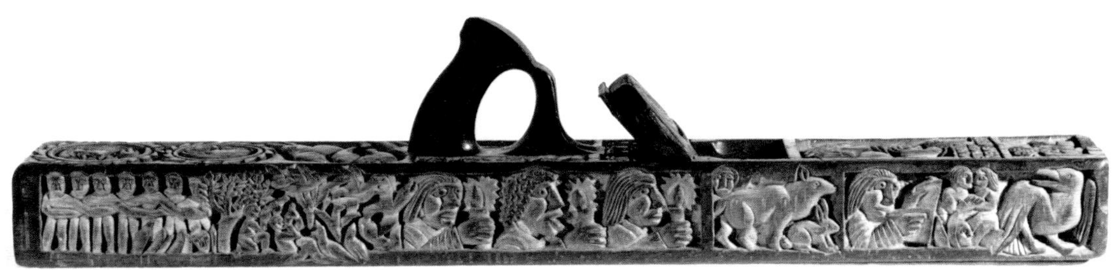

Save the Earth, 1986
2½ x 2½ x 30 inches
Wood
Courtesy of the artist
and Patricia Hamilton,
New York

ROBERT GRAHAM

Born: Mexico City, 1938.
Studied at San Jose State College, 1961-1963.
Attended San Francisco Art Institute, 1963-1964.

SELECTED ONE-PERSON EXHIBITIONS

1966 Nicholas Wilder Gallery, Los Angeles. Also shows in 1967, 1969, 1974, 1975, and 1977.

1968 Galerie Neuendorf, Hamburg/Cologne, West Germany. Also shows in 1970, 1974, 1976, and 1979.
Kornblee Gallery, New York.

1970 Whitechapel Gallery, London.

1971 Sonnabend Gallery, New York.

1972 Dallas Museum of Fine Arts.

1977 Robert Miller Gallery, New York. Also shows in 1978, 1979, and 1982.

1978 Los Angeles County Museum of Art.

1981 School of Visual Arts Museum, New York.
Walker Art Center, Minneapolis. Traveled to Norton Gallery and School of Art, West Palm Beach, Florida; The Museum of Fine Arts, Houston; Joslyn Art Museum, Omaha; Des Moines Art Center; San Francisco Museum of Modern Art.

1985 Robert Graham Studio, Venice, California.

SELECTED BIBLIOGRAPHY

Beal, Graham W.J. *Robert Graham Statues*. Exhibition Catalogue. Minneapolis: Walker Art Center, 1981.

Glazebrook, Mark. *Robert Graham*. Exhibition Catalogue. London: Whitechapel Gallery, 1970.

Isenberg, Barbara. "Robert Graham: Ignoring the Lessons of Modern Art." *ARTnews* (January 1979):66-69.

Murdock, Robert. *Robert Graham*. Exhibition Catalogue. Dallas: Dallas Museum of Fine Arts, 1972.

Ratcliff, Carter. *Robert Graham, Studies for the Olympic Gateway*. Exhibition Catalogue. Los Angeles: ARCO Center for the Visual Arts.

Tuchman, Maurice. *Robert Graham: Five Statues*. Exhibition Catalogue. Los Angeles: Los Angeles County Museum of Art, 1982.

Tuchman, Phyllis. "Artist's Dialogue, A Conversation with Robert Graham." *Architectural Digest* (October 1983):112-125.

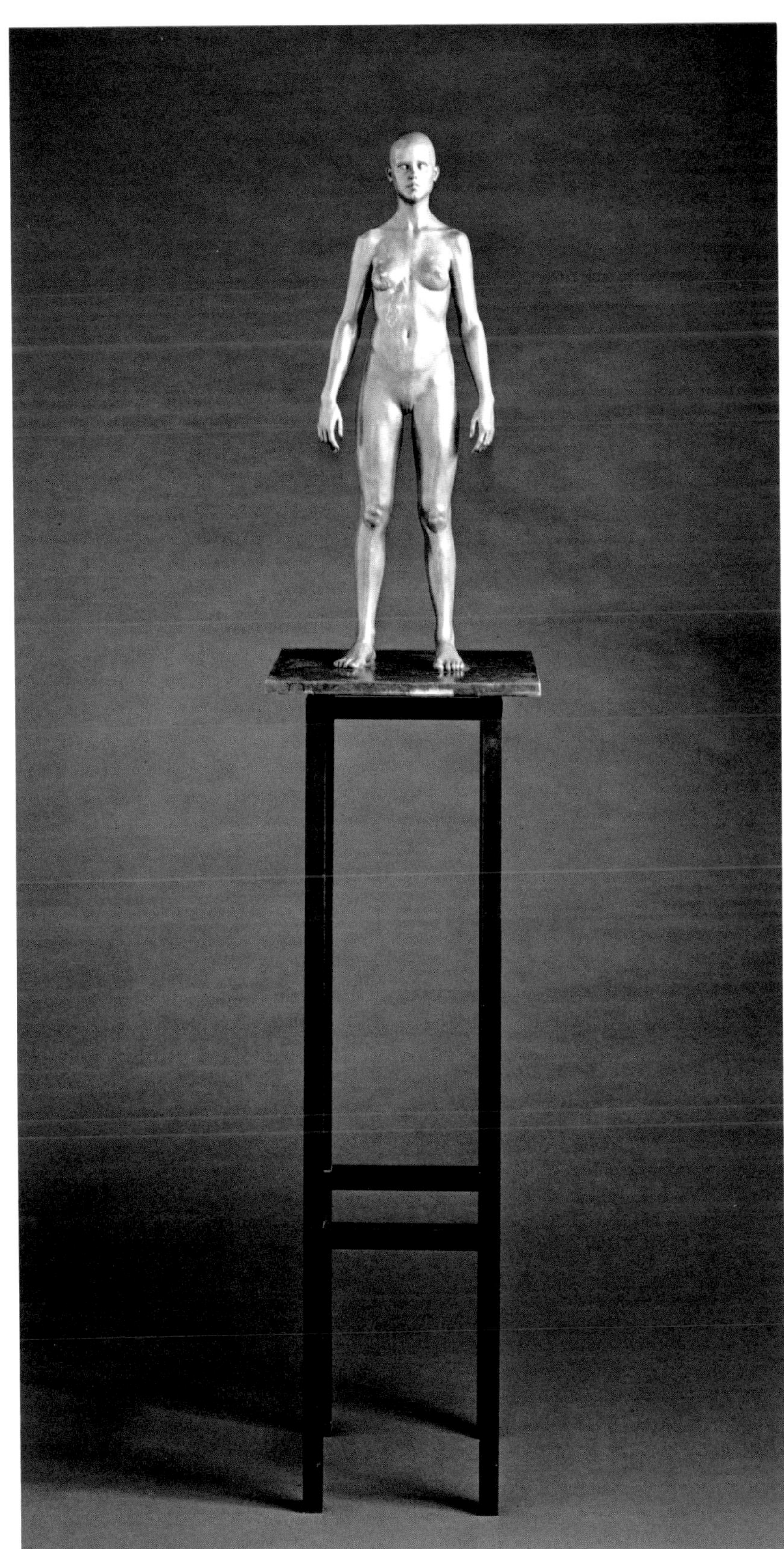

Lise I, 1977
67 x 10 x 6 inches
Bronze
Los Angeles County
Museum of Art,
purchased with
Matching Funds of
the National Endow-
ment for the Arts and
Mr. and Mrs. Morley
Benjamin

NANCY GRAVES

Born: Pittsfield, Massachusetts, 1940.
B.A., Vassar College, 1961.
B.F.A. and M.F.A., School of Art and Architecture, Yale University, 1964.

SELECTED ONE-PERSON EXHIBITIONS

1964 The Berkshire Museum, Pittsfield, Massachusetts.
1969 Whitney Museum of American Art, New York.
1971 Neue Galerie in Alten Kurhaus, Aachen, West Germany.
The Museum of Modern Art, New York.
1972 Institute of Contemporary Art of the University of Pennsylvania, Philadelphia. Traveled to Contemporary Arts Center, Cincinnati.
Janie C. Lee Gallery, Dallas, Texas. Also shows in 1973, 1974, 1975, 1977, 1978, 1983, and 1984.
1973 The Berkshire Museum, Pittsfield, Massachusetts.
La Jolla Museum of Contemporary Art. Traveled to Art Museum of South Texas, Corpus Christi.
1978 M. Knoedler and Company, Inc., New York. Also shows in 1979, 1980, 1981, 1982, 1984, 1985, 1986, and 1987.
1980 Albright-Knox Art Gallery, Buffalo. Traveled to Akron Art Institute, Ohio; Contemporary Arts Museum, Houston; Neuberger Museum, State University of New York, Purchase; Des Moines Art Center; Walker Art Center, Minneapolis.
1986 Vassar College Art Gallery, Poughkeepsie, New York. Traveled to The Berkshire Museum, Pittsfield, and The David Bell Gallery, List Art Center, Brown University, Providence, Rhode Island.
1987 Hirshhorn Museum and Sculpture Garden, Washington, D.C. Traveled to Fort Worth Art Museum; Santa Barbara Museum of Art; The Brooklyn Museum. Organized by Fort Worth Art Museum.

SELECTED BIBLIOGRAPHY

Amayo, Mario. "A Conversation with Nancy Graves." *Architectural Digest* (February 1982):146-155.
Balken, Debra Bricker. *Painting, Sculpture, Drawing 1980-1985*. Exhibition Catalogue. Pittsfield: The Berkshire Museum, 1986.
Berman, Avis. "Nancy Graves' New Age of Bronze." *ARTnews* (February 1986):56-64.
Carmean, E.A., Jr., Linda L. Cathcart, Robert Hughes, Michael Shapiro. *The Sculpture of Nancy Graves: A Catalogue Raisonné*. Doubles as Exhibition Catalogue for show organized at the Fort Worth Art Museum. New York: Hudson Hills Press, in association with Fort Worth Art Museum, 1987.
Cassidy, Martin W., Phyllis Tuchman, Elaine L. Johnson, and Nancy Graves. *Nancy Graves: Sculpture/Drawings/Films 1969-1971*. Exhibition Catalogue. Aachen, West Germany: Neue Galerie in Alten Kurhaus, 1971.
Cathcart, Linda L. *Nancy Graves: A Survey 1969/1980*. Exhibition Catalogue. Buffalo: Albright-Knox Art Gallery, 1980.
Frank, Elizabeth. "Her Own Way: The Daring and Inventive Sculptures of Nancy Graves." *Connoisseur* (February 1986):54-61.
Nancy Graves: Sculpture and Drawings, 1970-1972. Exhibition Catalogue. Philadelphia: Institute of Contemporary Art, 1972.
Shapiro, Michael Edward. "Nature into Sculpture: Nancy Graves and the Tradition of Direct Casting." *Arts Magazine* (November 1984):92-96.
Tuchman, Phyllis. *Nancy Graves: Painting and Sculpture 1978/82*. Exhibition Catalogue. Santa Barbara: Santa Barbara Contemporary Arts Forum, 1983.

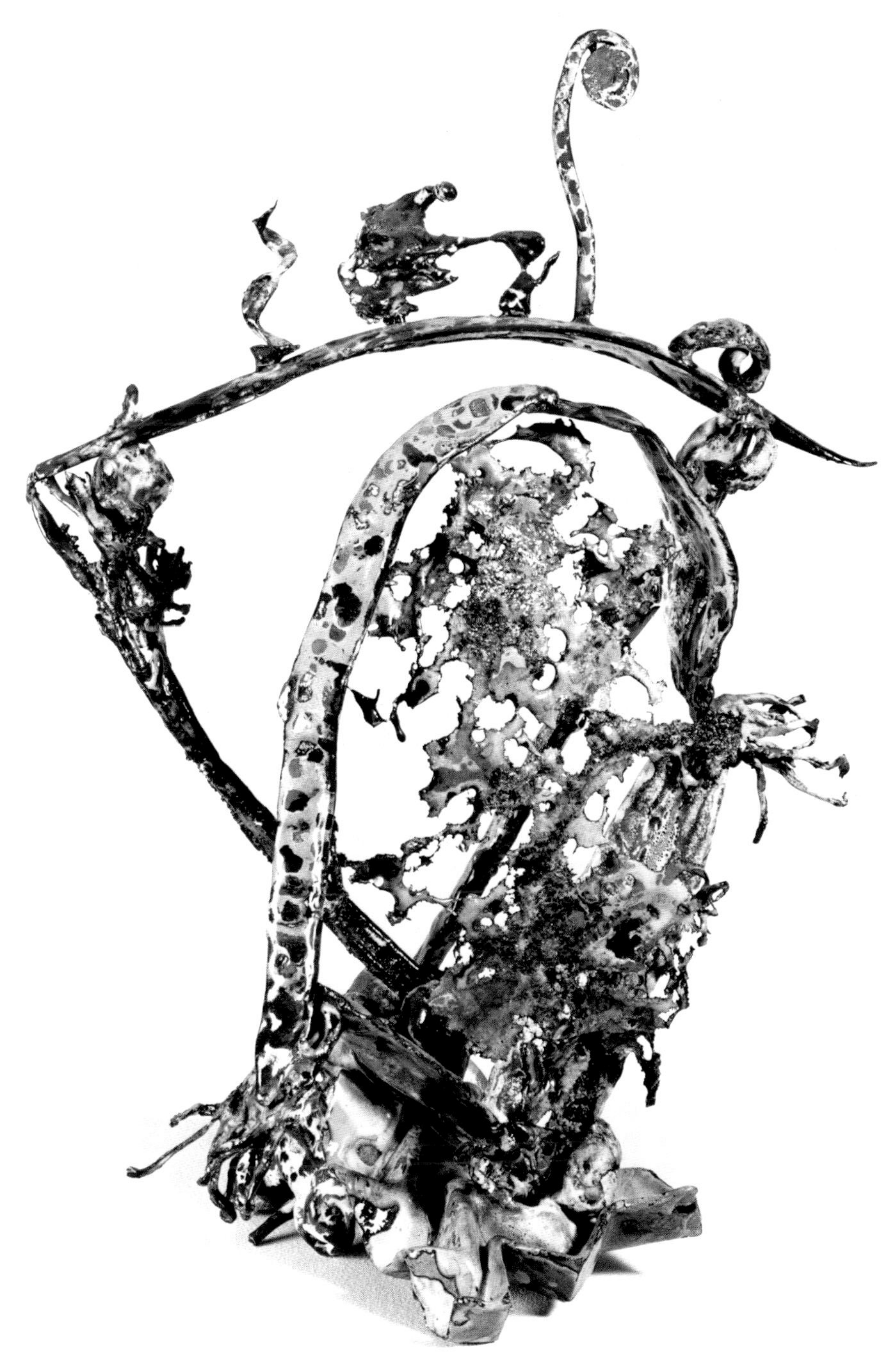

Janus, 1984
20¾ x 15¼ x 10 inches
Baked enamel on
bronze
Private Collection,
Courtesy M. Knoedler
and Co., Inc., New York
Photo: Ken Cohen

BRYAN HUNT

Born: Terre Haute, Indiana, 1947.
B.F.A,, Otis Art Institute of Los Angeles, 1969-71.
Whitney Museum of American Art, Independent Study Program, 1972.

SELECTED ONE-PERSON EXHIBITIONS

1974 The Institute for Art and Urban Resources, The Clocktower, New York.
1975 Palais des Beaux-Arts, Brussels.
1977 Blum Helman Gallery, New York. Also shows in 1978, 1979, 1981, 1983, 1985, 1986, and 1987.
1980 Margo Leavin Gallery, Los Angeles. Also show in 1983.
1981 Akron Art Institute, Ohio.
1983 Los Angeles County Museum of Art.
Amerika-Haus, West Berlin.
1985 M. Knoedler and Company, Zurich.
1986 University Art Museum, University of California, Berkeley.

SELECTED BIBLIOGRAPHY

Bryan Hunt, Recent Small-Scale Sculpture. Exhibition Catalogue. New York: Blum Helman Gallery, 1986.

Glenn, Constance W. "A Conversation with Bryan Hunt." *Architectural Digest* (March 1983):68-74.

__________, and Jane K. Bledsoe. *Bryan Hunt, A Decade of Drawings*. Exhibition Catalogue. Long Beach: Long Beach Art Museum, California State University, 1983.

Haskell, Barbara. *Bryan Hunt Skulpturen und Zeichnungen*. Exhibition Catalogue. Zurich: Knoedler, 1984-1985.

__________. *Bryan Hunt*. West Berlin: Amerika-Haus, 1983.

Ratcliff, Carter. *Bryan Hunt*. Exhibition Catalogue. New York: Blum Helman Gallery, 1983.

Saltz, Jerry. *Bryan Hunt*. Exhibition Catalogue. New York: Blum Helman Gallery, 1987.

Tuchman, Phyllis. "Bryan Hunt's Balancing Act." *ARTnews* (October 1985):65-73, cover.

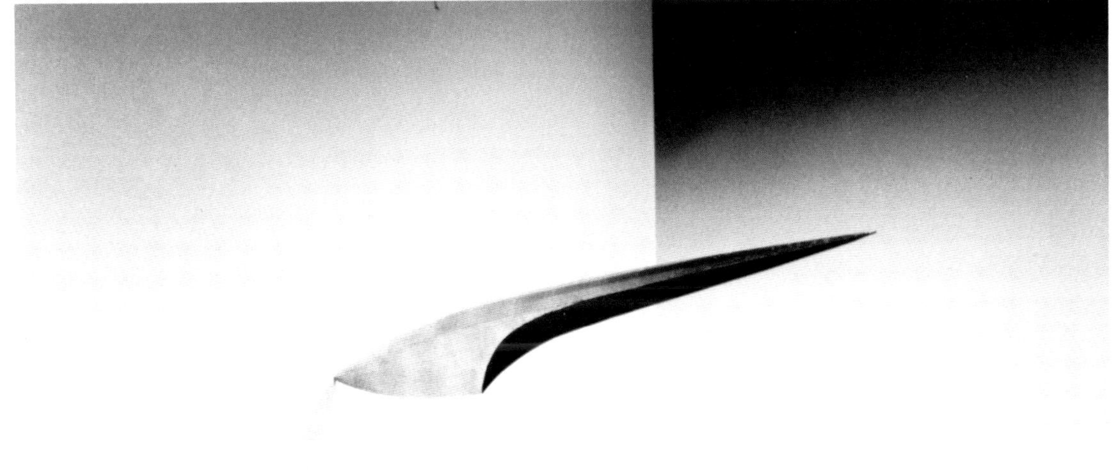

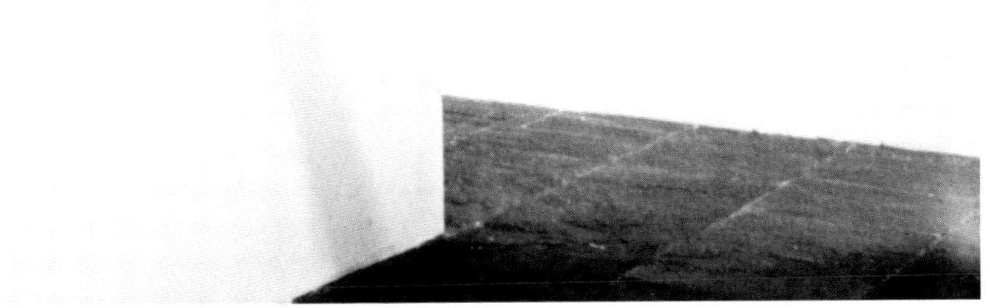

Nineteen Hundred Eighty-six, 1980
9 x 65 x 9 inches
Mixed media
Collection of Barbara
Haskell and Leon
Botstein, Courtesy
Blum Helman Gallery
Photo: Jon Abbott

MEL
KENDRICK

Born: Boston, 1949.
B.A., Trinity College, Hartford, Connecticut, 1971.
M.A., Hunter College, New York, 1973.

SELECTED ONE-PERSON EXHIBITIONS

1974 Artist's Space, New York.
1980 John Weber Gallery, New York.
Also shows in 1983, 1985, and 1987.
1983 Margo Leavin Gallery, Los Angeles.
Also show in 1985.
1986 University Gallery, University of Massachusetts, Amherst. Traveled to Contemporary Arts Museum, Houston; Neuberger Museum, State University of New York, Purchase.
Barbara Krakow Gallery, Boston.
1987 St. Louis Art Museum.

SELECTED BIBLIOGRAPHY

Klein, Michael R. *Mel Kendrick Sculpture*. Exhibition Catalogue. Storrs, Connecticut: Jorgensen Gallery, University of Connecticut, 1981.
Raynor, Vivian. "Sculpture: Mel Kendrick." *New York Times* (April 15, 1983).
Saunders, Wade. "Mel Kendrick at John Weber." *Art in America* (Summer 1983):155-156.
_____________. "Talking Objects: Interviews with Ten Younger Sculptors." *Art in America* (November 1985):123.
Siersma, Betsy. *Mel Kendrick Recent Sculpture*. Exhibition Catalogue. Amherst, Massachusetts: University Gallery, University of Massachusetts, 1986.
Tuchman, Phyllis. *Biederman/Gummer/Kendrick*. Exhibition Catalogue. Chicago: The Arts Club of Chicago, 1982.

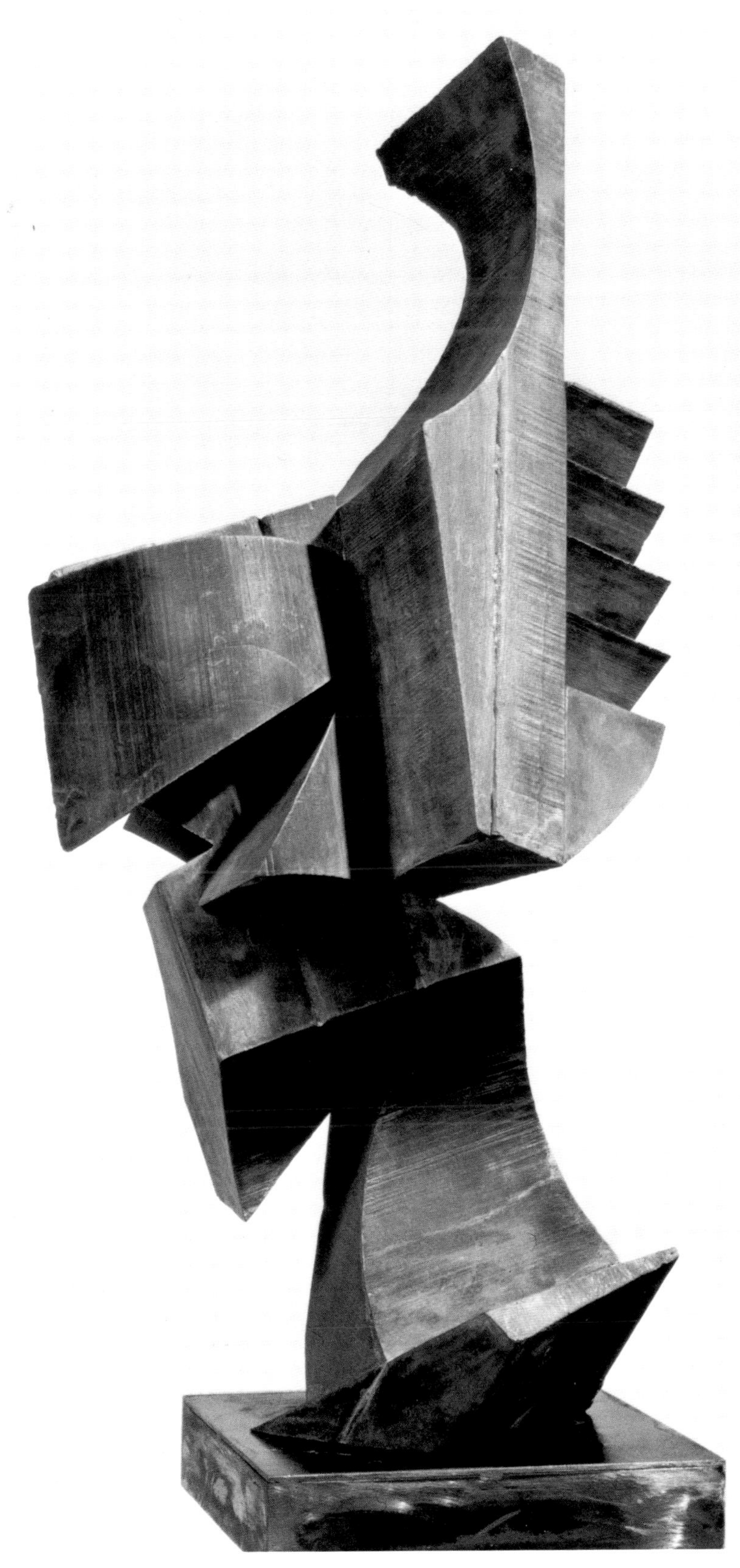

Five Piece Purple Heart,
1982-1985
29 x 12½ x 11 inches
Bronze
Collection of the artist

MICHAEL McMILLEN

Born: Los Angeles, 1946.
B.A., San Fernando Valley State College, 1969.
M.A., University of California, Los Angeles, 1972.
M.F.A., University of California, Los Angeles, 1973.

SELECTED ONE-PERSON EXHIBITIONS

1977 Los Angeles County Museum of Art, California. Traveled to Whitney Museum of American Art, New York.
1980 Art Gallery of New South Wales, Sydney, Australia.
Asher/Faure Gallery, Los Angeles. Also shows in 1982, 1984, and 1985.
1981 Pittsburgh Center for the Arts.
1985 Mills College Art Gallery, Oakland.
Installations, San Diego.
1986 112 Green Street Gallery with Patricia Hamilton, New York. Also show in 1987.
Laguna Art Museum/South Coast Plaza Site, Costa Mesa.
1987 Northridge Art Gallery, California State University.
Dart Gallery, Chicago.

SELECTED BIBLIOGRAPHY

Clothier, Peter. "Michael C. McMillen." *Art in America* (January 1983):127-128.
Larsen, Susan C. *Standing Alone in the Twilight*. Exhibition Catalogue. New York: Patricia Hamilton, 1986.
Perlberg, Deborah. "Michael McMillen." *Artforum* (December 1978):66-67.
Wortz, Melinda. "Inner City of the Mind." *ARTnews* (February 1978):106, 108.

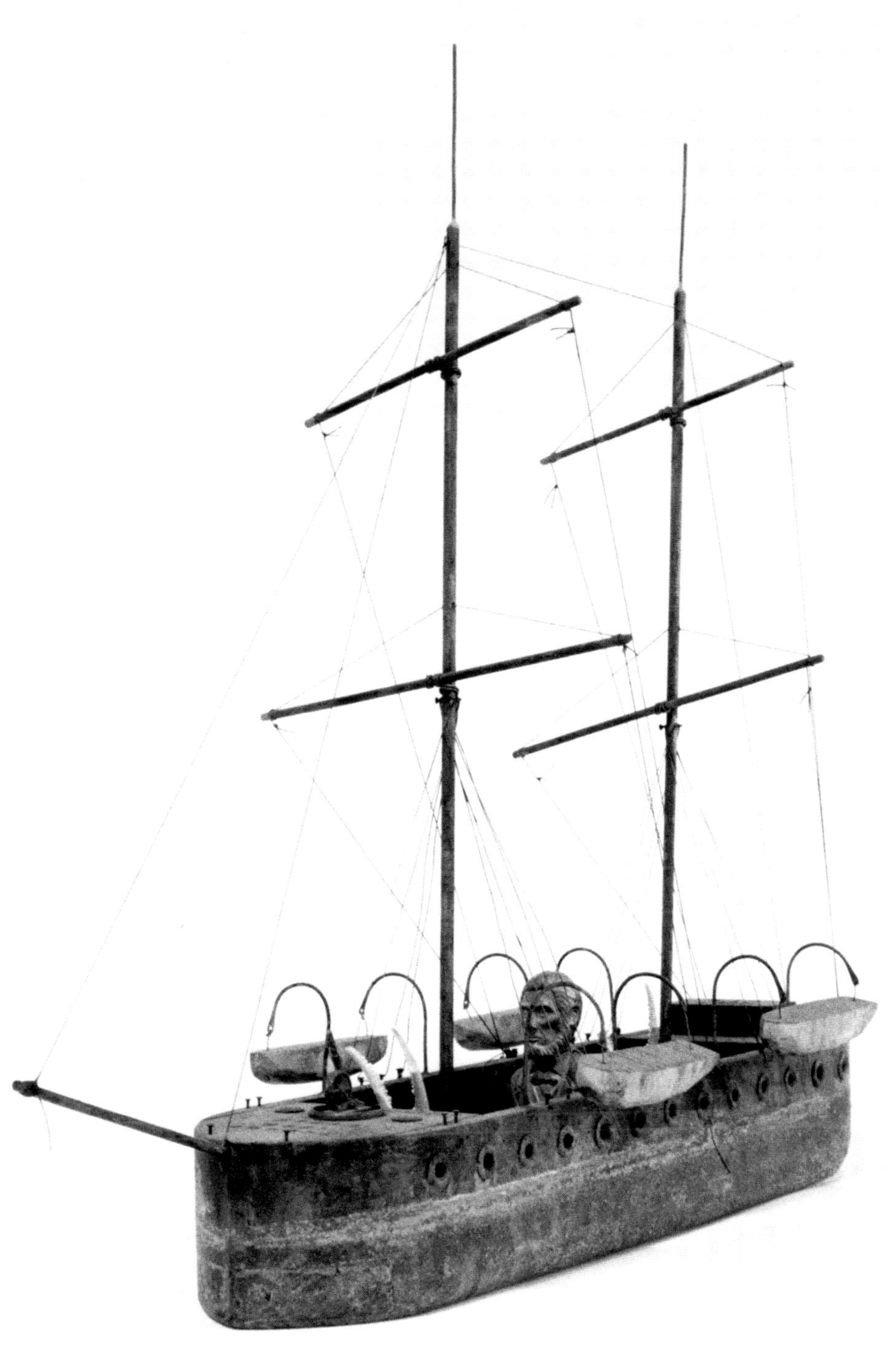

Pequod, 1985
16¼ x 6¾ x 19½ inches
Wood, metal, mirror,
crab claws
Collection of the artist

TOM
OTTERNESS

Born: Wichita, Kansas, 1952.
Art Students League, New York, 1970.
Independent Study Program, Whitney Museum of American Art, New York, 1973.

SELECTED ONE-PERSON EXHIBITIONS

1983 Brooke Alexander, Inc., New York. Also shows in 1985 and 1987.
1984 Galerie Rudolf Zwirner, Cologne, West Germany.
1986 Three Rivers Arts Festival, Pittsburgh.
1987 The Museum of Modern Art, New York.

SELECTED BIBLIOGRAPHY

Blau, Douglas. "New York: Tom Otterness at Brooke Alexander." *Art in America* (March 1983):149-150.
Clark, Vicky A. *The World According to Tom Otterness*. Exhibition Catalogue. Pittsburgh: Three Rivers Arts Festival, 1986.
Robinson, Walter. "Arcadian Hijinks." *Art in America* (December 1985):94-97.
Russi-Kirschner, Judith. "Tom Otterness' Frieze." *Artforum* (October 1983):57-60.
Shearer, Linda. *Projects: Tom Otterness*. Exhibition Brochure. New York: The Museum of Modern Art, 1987.

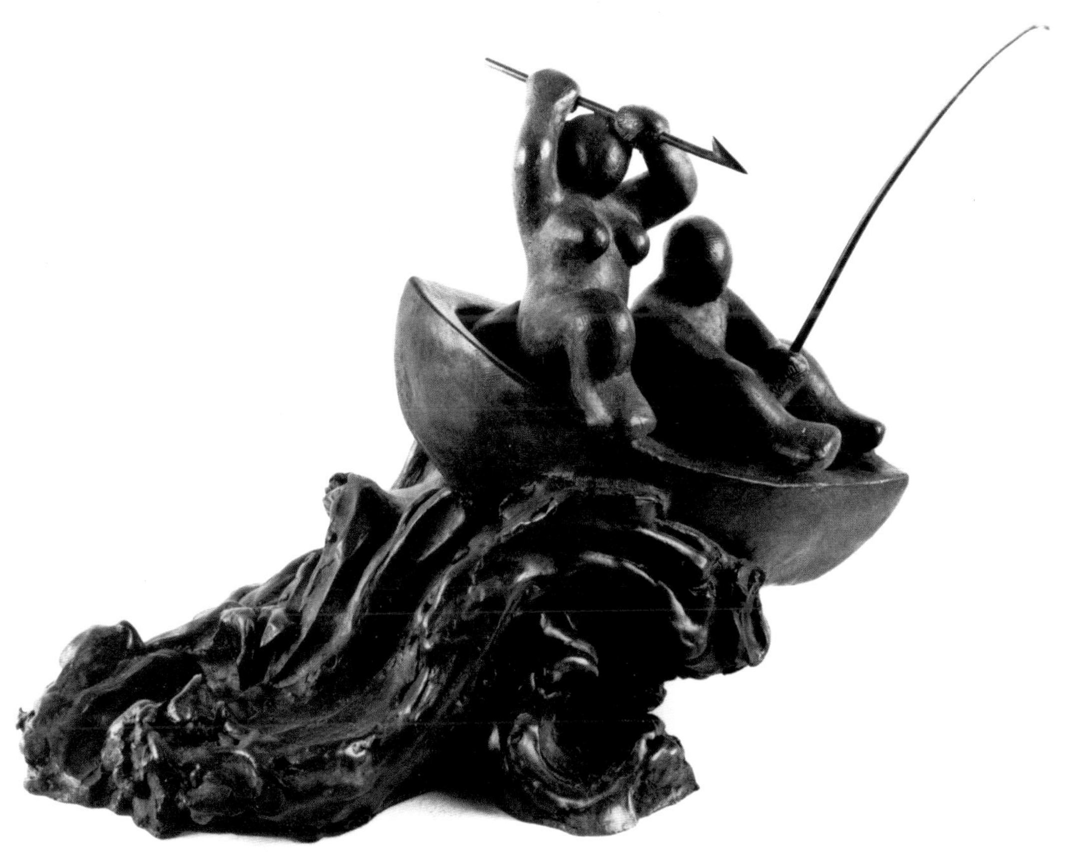

Boat with Wave,
1986-1987
11½ x 11 x 9 inches
Bronze
Courtesy Brooke
Alexander Gallery,
New York
Photo: Ivan Dalla Tana

BEVERLY PEPPER

Born: New York City, 1924.
Studied at Pratt Institute.
Studied at Art Students League, New York.
Honorary Degrees: Doctor of Fine Arts, Pratt Institute, 1982; Doctor of Fine Arts, The Maryland Institute, 1983.

SELECTED ONE-PERSON EXHIBITIONS

1969 Marlborough Gallery, New York.
The Jewish Museum, New York.
Museum of Contemporary Art, Chicago.

1975 Andre Emmerich Gallery, New York. Also shows in 1977, 1979, 1981, 1982, 1983, 1984, 1986, and 1987.

1976 San Francisco Museum of Art.

1977 Seattle Art Museum, Washington.
Indianapolis Museum of Art, Indiana. Also show in 1978.

1979 Piazza Mostra, Todi, Perugia, Italy.

1986 Albright-Knox Art Gallery, Buffalo. Traveled to San Francisco Museum of Modern Art; Columbus Museum of Art; The Brooklyn Museum, New York; Center for the Fine Arts, Miami.

SELECTED BIBLIOGRAPHY

Abbodanza, Roberto, Sam Hunter, and Marisa Volpi Orlandini. *Beverly Pepper in Todi*. Perugia, Italy: Sculpture nella Piazza Mostra Todi, 1979.

Baker, Kenneth. "Interconnections: Beverly Pepper." *Art in America* (April 1984):176-179.

Cohen, Ronny. *Beverly Pepper*. Exhibition Catalogue. New York: Andre Emmerich Gallery, 1986.

Fry, Ed. *Beverly Pepper: Sculpture 1971-1975*. Exhibition Catalogue. San Francisco: Museum of Art, 1975.

Krauss, Rosalind. *Beverly Pepper: Sculpture in Place*. Doubles as Exhibition Catalogue for show organized at the Albright-Knox Art Gallery. New York: Abbeville Press, 1986.

Larson, Kay. "Hot Pepper." *New York* (June 8, 1987):46-58.

Sheffield, Margaret. "Beverly Pepper's New Sculpture." *ARTS Magazine* (September 1979):172-173.

Tuchman, Phyllis. *Beverly Pepper: The Moline Markers*. Exhibition Catalogue. Davenport, Iowa: Davenport Art Gallery, 1981.

Van der Marck, Jan. *Beverly Pepper, Recent Sculpture*. New York: Marlborough-Gerson Gallery, Inc., 1969.

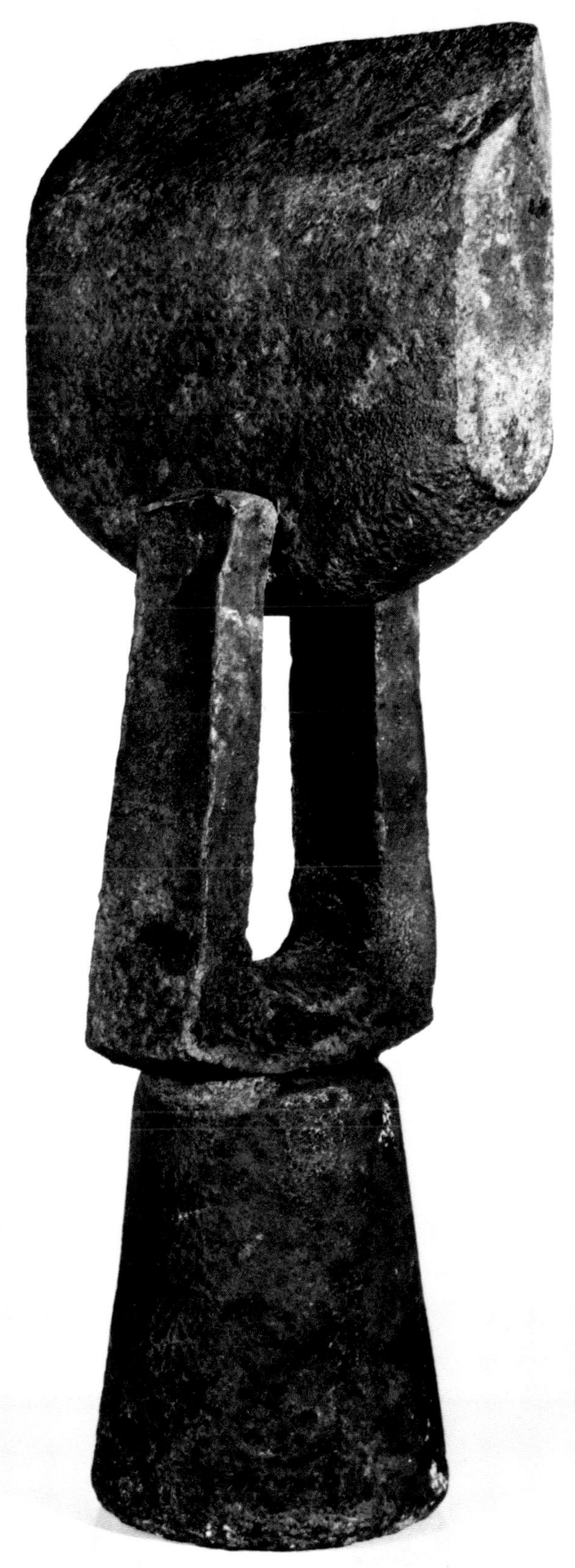

Goliath Wedge, 1978
22 x 8 x 5½ inches
Cast and forged iron
Albright-Knox Art
Gallery, Gift of
Seymour H. Knox
Photo: Courtesy The
Brooklyn Museum

KEN
PRICE

Born: Los Angeles, 1935.
Studied at Chouinard Art Institute and Los Angeles County Art Institute.
B.F.A., University of Southern California, 1956.
M.F.A., State University of New York, Alfred, 1959.

SELECTED ONE-PERSON EXHIBITIONS

1960 Ferus Gallery, Los Angeles. Also shows in 1961 and 1964.
1966 Los Angeles County Museum of Art.
1968 Kasmin Gallery, London. Also show in 1970.
1969 Whitney Museum of American Art, New York.
       Mizuno Gallery, Los Angeles. Also show in 1971.
1970 Gemini G.E.L., Los Angeles. Also show in 1972.
1974 Willard Gallery, New York. Also shows in 1979, 1982, 1984, and 1985.
1976 James Corcoran Gallery, Los Angeles. Also shows in 1980 and 1982.
1978 Los Angeles County Museum of Art.
       Gallery of Contemporary Art, New Mexico.
1980 Contemporary Arts Museum, Houston.
       Visual Arts Museum, New York.
1983 Leo Castelli Gallery, New York.

SELECTED BIBLIOGRAPHY

Cathcart, Linda L. *Ken Price: Selections from Happy's Curios*. Exhibition
    Catalogue. Houston: Contemporary Arts Museum, 1980.
Coplans, John. "The Sculpture of Ken Price." *Art International* (March 1964):33-34.
Lippard, Lucy R. *Robert Irwin and Ken Price*. Exhibition Catalogue. Los Angeles:
    Los Angeles County Museum of Art, 1966.
Rose, Barbara. *Figurine Cups by Ken Price*. Exhibition Brochure. Los Angeles:
    Gemini G.E.L., 1970.
Schjeldahl, Peter. "Ken Price, Los Angeles County Museum." *Artforum*
    (November 1978):78-79.
Simon, Joan. "An Interview with Ken Price." *Art in America* (January 1980):98-104.
Tuchman, Maurice. *Ken Price: Happy's Curios*. Exhibition Catalogue. Los Angeles:
    Los Angeles County Museum of Art, 1978.

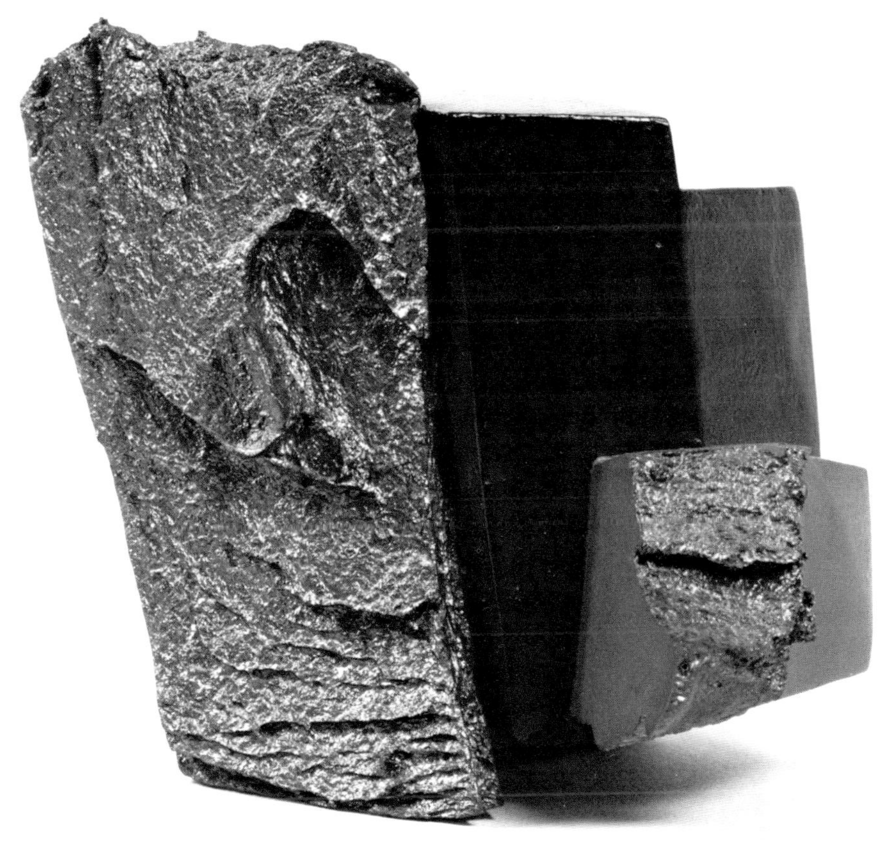

Turk, 1983
3¼ x 3¼ x 4½ inches
Ceramic and paint
Courtesy Charles
Cowles Gallery,
New York

PETER REGINATO

Born: Dallas, 1945.
Studied at San Francisco Art Institute, 1963-1966.

SELECTED ONE-PERSON EXHIBITIONS

1971 Tibor de Nagy Gallery, New York. Also shows in 1973 and 1975, and at Houston gallery in 1974, 1979, and 1980.
1981 Salander-O'Reilly Galleries, Inc., New York. Also shows in 1982 and 1983.
1983 New Jersey State Council on the Arts.
1985 112 Greene Street with Patricia Hamilton, New York. Also show in 1987.
1986 57th Street West Gallery with Patricia Hamilton, Los Angeles.

SELECTED BIBLIOGRAPHY

Carmean, E.A., Jr. "Peter Reginato." *Arts Magazine* (June 1978):26.

Firestone, Evan. *Three Musicians at the Harlequin's Carnival: Peter Reginato New Sculpture*. New York: Patricia Hamilton, 1985. Reprinted in: *Arts Magazine* (February 1985):116-119.

Frackman, Noel. "Peter Reginato." *Arts Magazine* (January 1978):5.

Monte, James. "Reginato's New Work." *Museum Magazine* (November/December 1981).

Towle, Tony. "Peter Reginato." *Art in America* (September 1985):130.

——————. "Peter Reginato at Tibor de Nagy." *Art in America* (September 1979):136.

Tuchman, Phyllis. *Sculptures of the Unexpected: Peter Reginato New Sculpture*. Los Angeles: Patricia Hamilton, 1986.

——————. "The Road Now Taken." *Art Criticism* (Vol. 2, 1986):22-25.

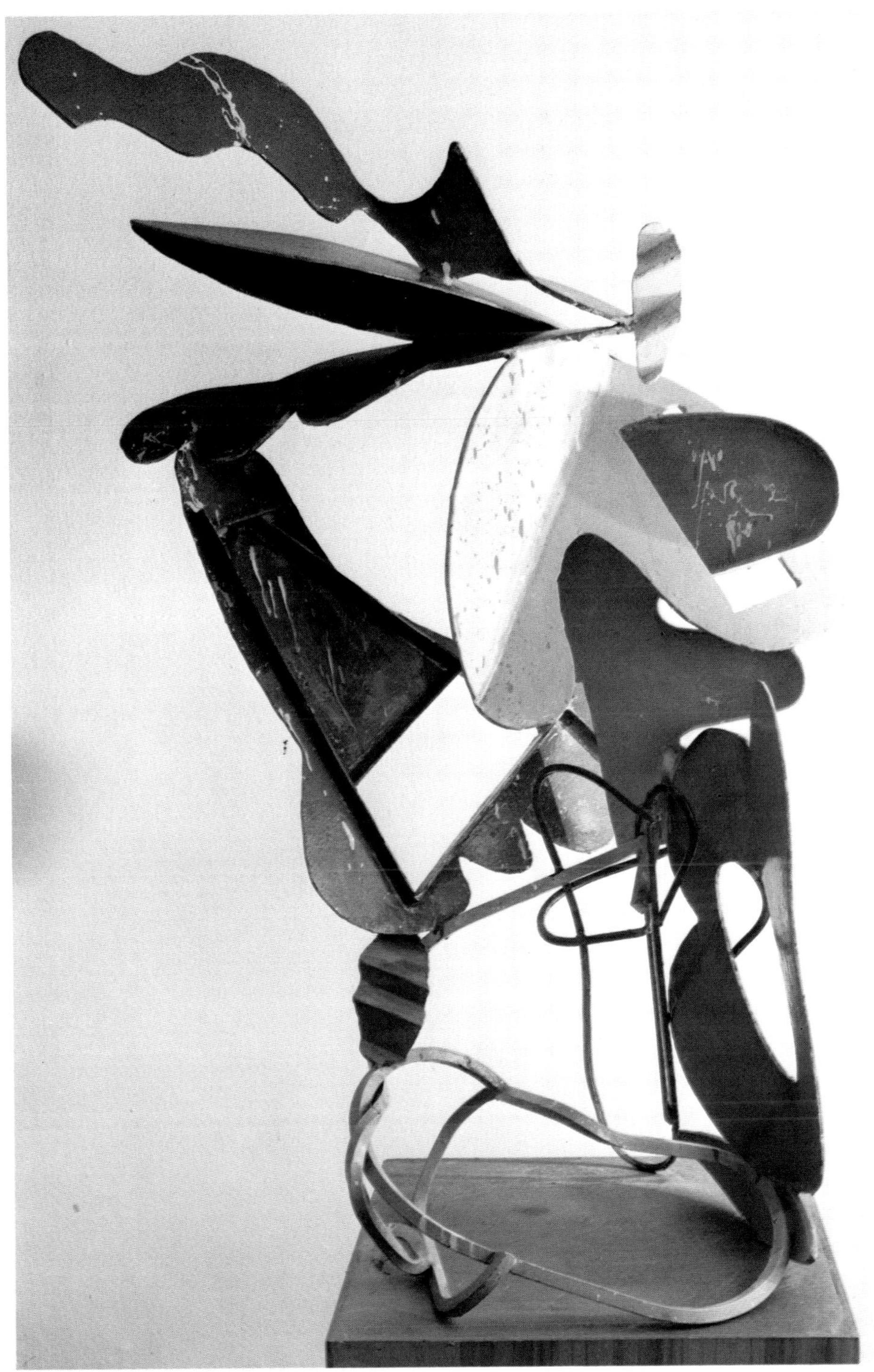

Manhattan Love Song,
1984
42 x 29 x 18 inches
Painted steel
Private collection,
New York

CLIFFORD
ROSS

Born: New York City, 1952.
Attended Skowhegan School of Painting and Sculpture, 1973.
B.A., Yale University, 1974.

SELECTED ONE-PERSON EXHIBITIONS

1976 Tibor de Nagy Gallery, New York. Also show in 1978.
1977 William Edward O'Reilly, Inc., New York.
1979 Byck Gallery, Louisville, Kentucky.
Watson-De Nagy Gallery, Houston.
1980 Salander-O'Reilly Galleries, Inc., New York. Also show in 1984.

SELECTED BIBLIOGRAPHY

Frank, Peter. "To Be Young, Gifted, and Avant-garde: III." *Village Voice* (July 10, 1978).
Goldberger, Paul. "Clifford Ross at Tibor de Nagy." *Art in America* (July/August 1979):117.
Perreault, John. "Clifford Ross." *The Soho News* (December 1, 1981).
Rogers, Connie. "Clifford Ross." *Arts Magazine* (January 1979):10.
Shapiro, Michael Edward. *Clifford Ross Sculpture and Paintings*. New York: Salander-O'Reilly Galleries, Inc., 1984.

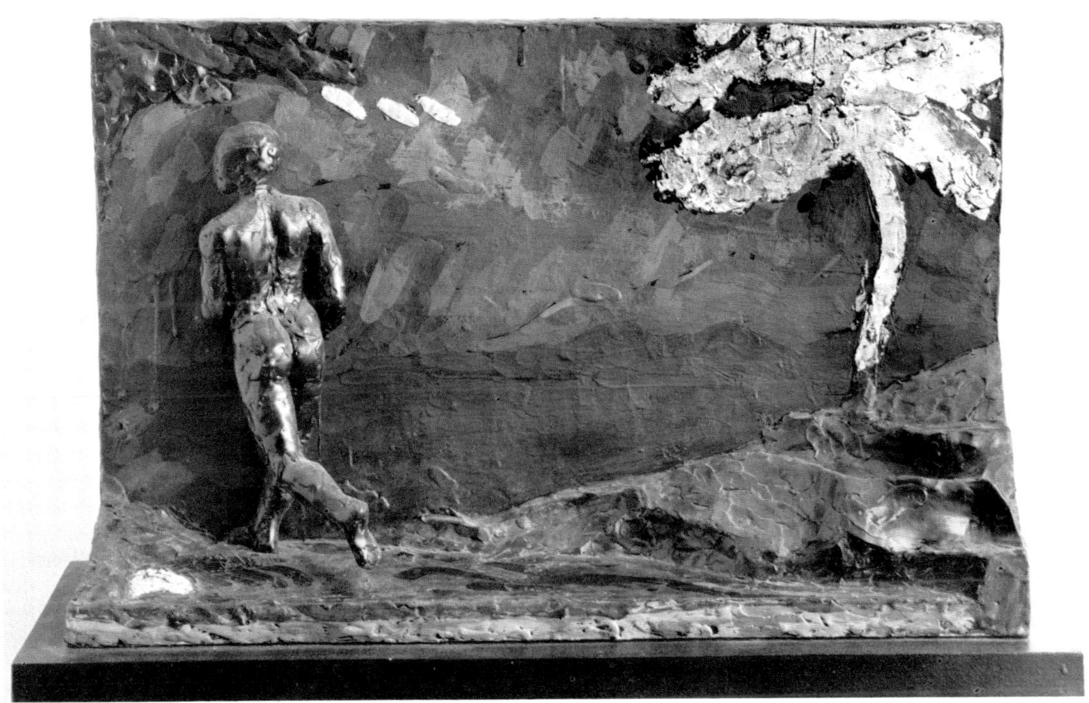

Running Man, 1984
14 x 23 x 6½ inches
Wax with encaustic,
oil paint, and gilt
Collection of the artist

<table>
<tr><td>

**LUCAS
SAMARAS**

</td><td>

Born: Kastoria, Macedonia, Greece, 1936.
Attended Rutgers University, 1955-1959.
Attended Columbia University, New York, 1960.

</td></tr>
</table>

SELECTED ONE-PERSON EXHIBITIONS

1962 Green Gallery, New York. Also show in 1964.
1966 The Pace Gallery, New York. Also shows in 1968, 1970, 1971, 1972, 1974, 1975, 1978, 1979, 1980, 1982, 1984, 1985, and 1987.
1969 The Museum of Modern Art, New York.
1970 Kunstverein Hannover, West Germany.
1971 Museum of Contemporary Art, Chicago.
1972 Whitney Museum of American Art, New York.
1975 The Museum of Modern Art, New York.
1976 Institute of Contemporary Art, Boston.
Seattle Art Museum Pavilion.
1977 Walker Art Center, Minneapolis.
1978 Akron Art Museum, Ohio.
1982 Denver Art Museum. Traveled to Lowe Art Museum, University of Miami, Coral Gables, Florida; Madison Art Center, Wisconsin; Walker Art Center, Minneapolis; Portland Art Museum, Oregon; Art Museum of South Texas, Corpus Christi; Institute of Contemporary Art, Boston.
1983 Centre Georges Pompidou, Paris. Traveled to Musée d'Art et d'Histoire, Fribourg, Switzerland; Frankfurter Kunstverein, Frankfurt, West Germany; Serpentine Gallery, London; International Center of Photography, New York; Center for Creative Photography, University of Arizona, Tuscon; Phoenix Art Museum; Krannert Art Museum, Champaign, Illinois; Lowe Art Museum, University of Miami, Coral Gables, Florida; Kennedy Gallery, Cambridge, Massachusetts; Photographic Research Center, Boston. Organized by the Polaroid International Collection.

SELECTED BIBLIOGRAPHY

Alloway, Lawrence. *Samaras: Selected Works 1960-1966*. Exhibition Catalogue. New York: Pace Gallery, 1966.

Blau, Douglas, and Lucas Samaras. *Lucas Samaras: Chairs, Heads, Panoramas*. New York: Pace Gallery, 1984.

Conrads, Margaret. "An Interview with Lucas Samaras." *Issue 2* (Winter 1985):8-12. In the same issue, "From the Diary of Lucas Samaras," pp. 13-15.

Glimcher, Arnold. "Lucas Samaras." *Flash Art* (October/November 1985):40-45.

Kuspit, Donald B. *Samaras: Pastels and Bronzes*. Exhibition Catalogue. New York: Pace Gallery, 1982.

Levin, Kim. "Eros, Samaras, and Recent Art." *Arts Magazine* (December 1972-January 1983):51-55.

___________. *Lucas Samaras*. New York: Harry N. Abrams, Inc., 1975.

Ratcliff, Carter. *Lucas Samaras: Sittings 1979-1980*. Exhibition Catalogue. New York: Pace Gallery, 1980.

Samaras, Lucas. *Chair Transformations*. Exhibition Catalogue. New York: Pace Gallery, 1970.

___________. *Lucas Samaras*. Exhibition Catalogue. New York: Whitney Museum of American Art, 1973.

Schjeldahl, Peter. *Samaras Pastels*. Denver: Denver Art Museum, 1981.

Schwartz, Sanford. "Lucas Samaras." *The Art Presence*. New York: Horizon Press, 1982: 130-141.

Solomon, Alan. "A Conversation with Lucas Samaras." *Artforum* (October 1966):39-44.

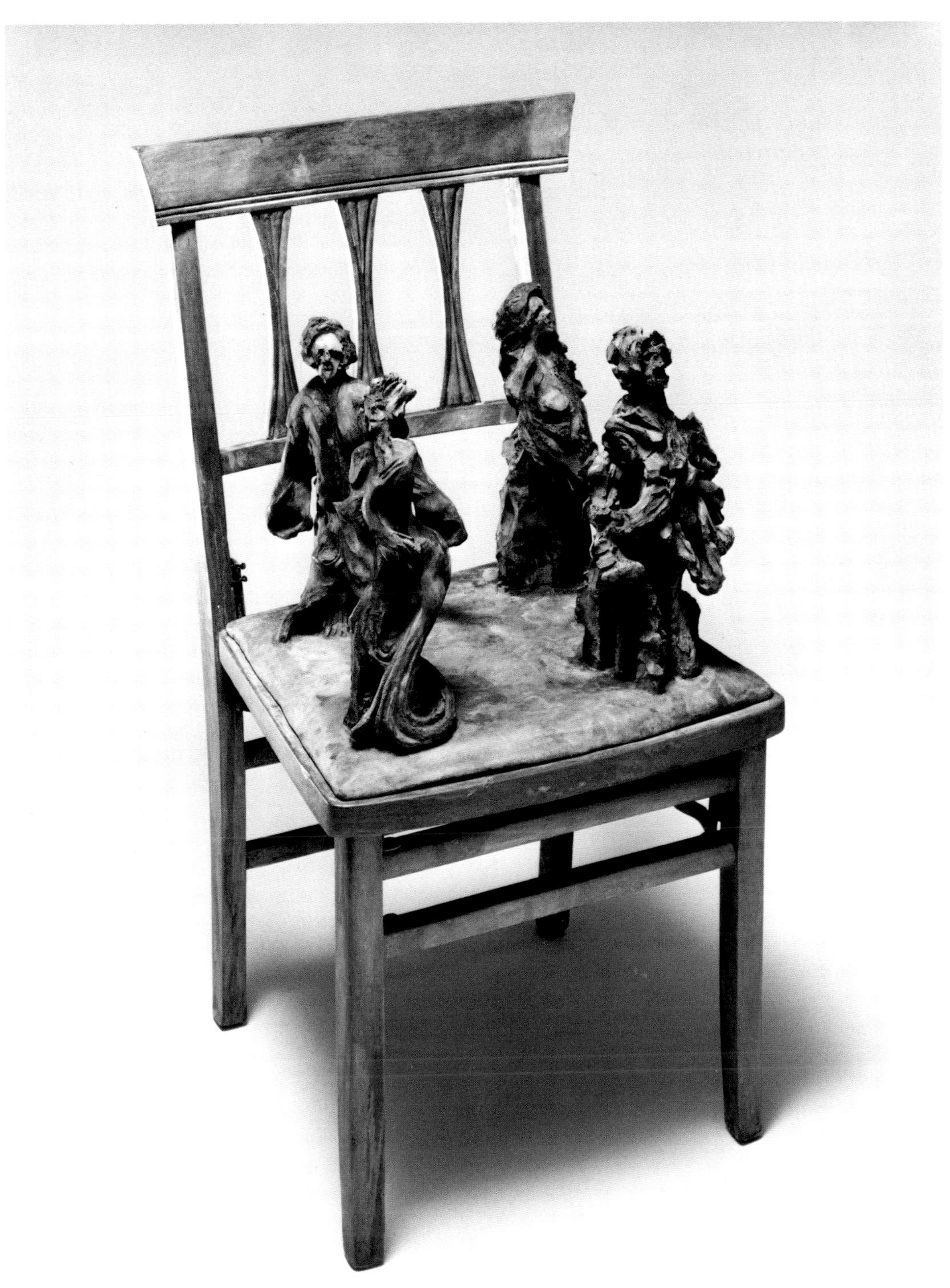

Chair with Four Figures,
1983
33 x 17½ x 19 inches
Bronze
Courtesy Pace Gallery,
New York
(not in exhibition)

JOEL SHAPIRO

Born: New York, 1941.
B.A., New York University, 1964.
M.A., New York University, 1969.

SELECTED ONE-PERSON EXHIBITIONS

1970 Paula Cooper Gallery, New York. Also shows in 1972, 1974, 1975, 1976, 1977, 1979, 1980, 1982, 1983, 1984, and 1986.
1976 Museum of Contemporary Art, Chicago.
1977 Max Protetch Gallery, Washington, D.C.
Albright-Knox Art Gallery, Buffalo.
1979 Akron Art Institute, Ohio.
1980 Whitechapel Art Gallery, London. Traveled to Museum Haus Lange, Krefeld, West Germany, and Moderna Museet, Stockholm.
Bell Gallery, Brown University, Providence, Rhode Island. Traveled to Georgia State University, Atlanta, and The Contemporary Arts Center, Cincinnati.
1982 Whitney Museum of American Art, New York. Traveled to Dallas Museum of Fine Arts; Art Gallery of Ontario, Toronto; La Jolla Museum of Contemporary Art.
1985 Stedelijk Museum, Amsterdam. Traveled to Kunstmuseum Düsseldorf and Staatliche Kunsthalle, Baden-Baden.
1986 Seattle Art Museum, Washington.
The John and Mable Ringling Museum of Art, Sarasota, Florida.

SELECTED BIBLIOGRAPHY

Baker, Kenneth. "Artist's Dialogue: More Motion, More Dislocation—The Art of Joel Shapiro." *Architectural Digest* (June 1984):170, 174, 176, 178.

Bass, Ruth. "Minimalism Made Human." *ARTnews* (March 1987):95-101.

Bear, Liza. "Joel Shapiro Torquing: A Dialogue with Liza Bear." *Avalanche* (Summer 1975):15-19.

Bloem, Marja, and Karel Schampers. *Joel Shapiro*. Exhibition Catalogue. Amsterdam: Stedelijk Museum, 1985.

Coplans, John. "Joel Shapiro: An Interview." *Dialogue* (January/February 1979):7-9.

Krauss, Rosalind. *Joel Shapiro*. Exhibition Catalogue. Chicago: Museum of Contemporary Art, 1976.

Kuspit, Donald B. "Manifest Destinies." *Art in America* (May 1983):148-152.

Marshall, Richard, and Roberta Smith. *Joel Shapiro*. Exhibition Catalogue. New York: Whitney Museum of American Art, 1985.

Ormond, Mark. *Joel Shapiro: Sculpture and Drawings, 1981-1985*. Exhibition Catalogue. Sarasota, Florida: John and Mable Ringling Museum of Art, 1986.

Schwartz, Sanford. "Little Big Sculpture." *Art in America* (March/April, 1976):53-55. Reprinted in *The Art Presence*, New York, Horizon Press, 1982:72-76.

Smith, Roberta. *Joel Shapiro*. Exhibition Catalogue. London: Whitechapel Gallery, 1980.

Tuchman, Phyllis. "Shapiro: Redirecting Sculpture's Shapes." *New York Newsday* (November 28, 1986).

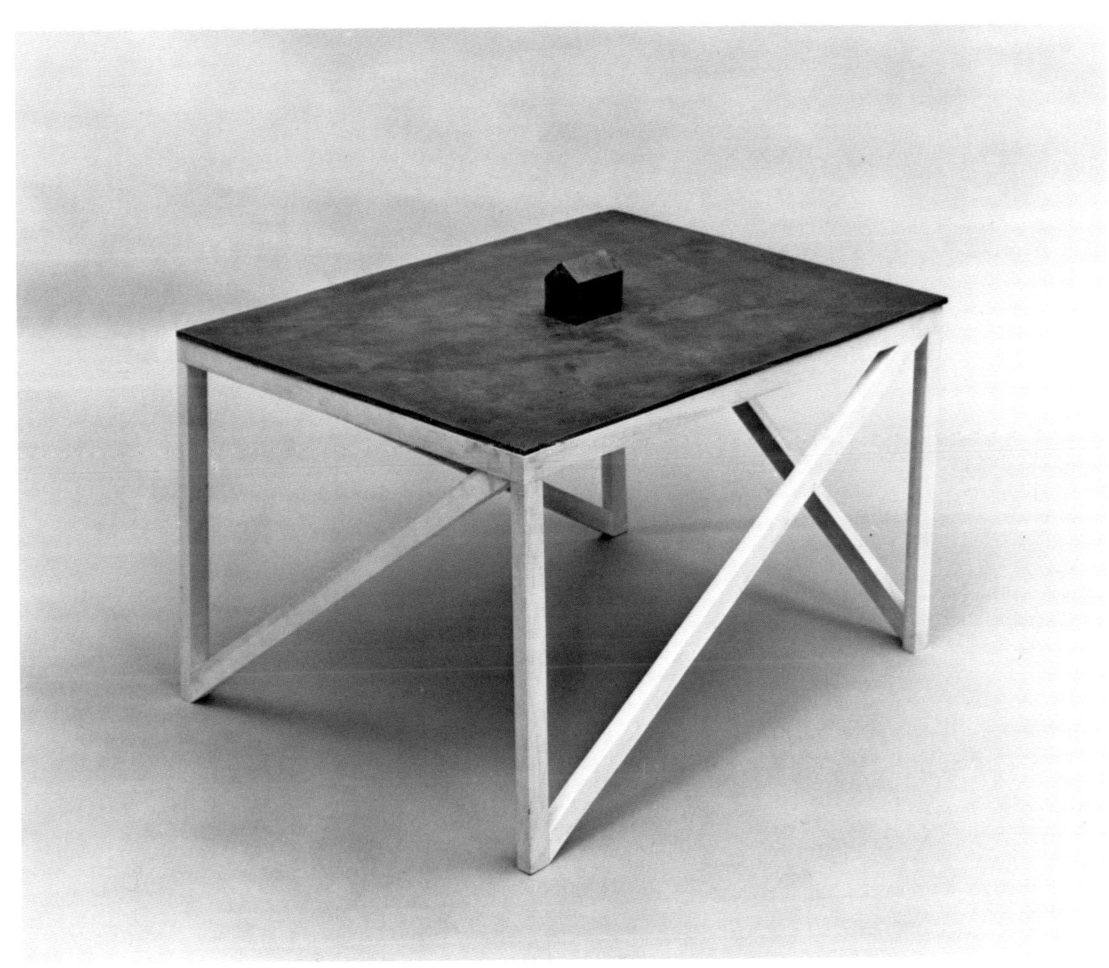

untitled, 1975-1976
3½ x 21⅛ x 28¾ inches
Bronze
Collection of the artist.
Photo: Courtesy Paula
Cooper Gallery

CHARLES
SIMONDS

Born: New York, 1945.
B.A., University of California, Berkeley, 1967.
M.F.A., Rutgers University, 1969

SELECTED ONE-PERSON EXHIBITIONS

1975 Centre National d'Art Contemporain, Paris.
1976 The Museum of Modern Art, New York.
1977 Albright-Knox Art Gallery, Buffalo.
1978 Bonner Kunstverein, Bonn.
1979 Wallraf-Richartz Museum, Cologne.
      Nationalgalerie, Berlin.
1981 Museum of Contemporary Art, Chicago.
      Solomon R. Guggenheim Museum, New York.
1984 Leo Castelli Gallery, New York.
1985 Architekturmuseum, Basel.
1986 Galerie Maeght Lelong, Paris.

SELECTED BIBLIOGRAPHY

Beardsley, John. "Extending the Metaphor." *Art International* (February 1979):14-19.
Castle, Ted. "Charles Simonds: The New Adam." *Art in America* (February
      1983):94-103.
Cathcart, Linda L., and D. Abadie. *Charles Simonds*. Exhibition Catalogue. Buffalo:
      Albright-Knox Art Gallery, 1977.
Linker, Kate. "Charles Simonds' Emblematic Architecture." *Artforum* (March
      1979):32-37.
Patton, Phil. "The Lost Worlds of the 'Little People'." *ARTnews* (February
      1983):84-90.
Simonds, Charles. "Working in the Streets of Shanghai and Guilin." *Artforum*
      (Summer 1980):60-61.

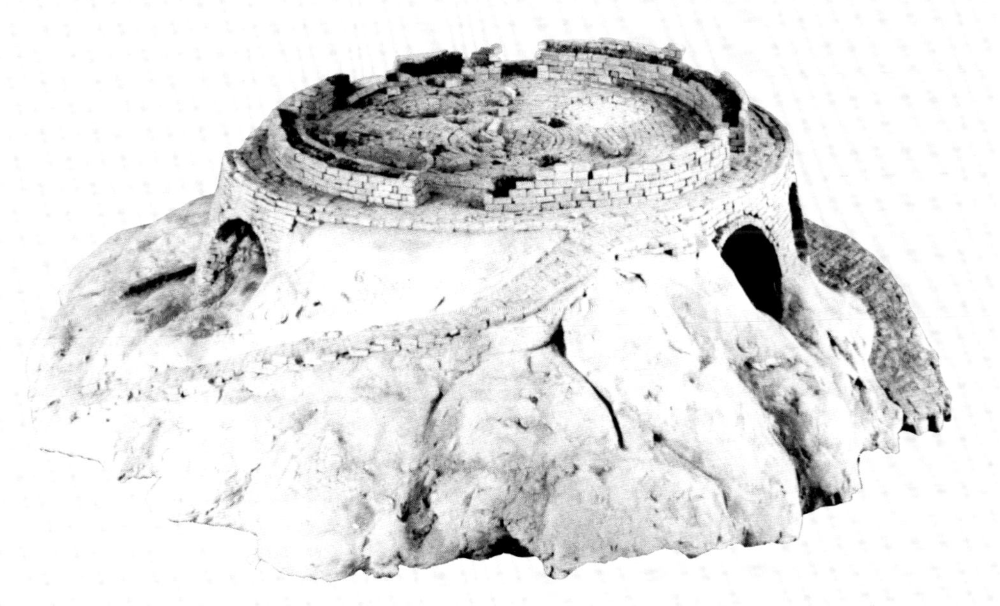

Kiln, circa 1972
7 x 24 x 21 inches
Unfired clay, clay
powder, lumps of
charcoal and dried
moss
Collection of Monique
and Foster Goldstrom
Photo: Courtesy
Christies, New York

JAMES WOLFE

Born: New York, 1944.

SELECTED ONE-PERSON EXHIBITIONS

1973 Andre Emmerich, New York. Also shows in 1974, 1975, 1976, 1977, 1985, and 1986.
1978 Meredith Long Contemporary, New York. Also show in 1979.
1981 Virginia Polytechnic Institute and State University, Blacksburg, Virginia.
1986 The Phillips Collection, Washington, D.C.
1987 Galerie Wentzel, Cologne.
Rubiner Gallery, West Bloomfield, Michigan.

SELECTED BIBLIOGRAPHY

Brenson, Michael. "James Wolfe." *New York Times* (November 11, 1983):C30.
Raynor, Vivian. "James Wolfe." *New York Times* (April 12, 1985):C26.
Tatransky, Valentin. "James Wolfe." *Arts Magazine* (January 1984):54.
Wilkin, Karen. "James Wolfe's New Sculpture." *Arts Magazine* (April 1985):114-115.

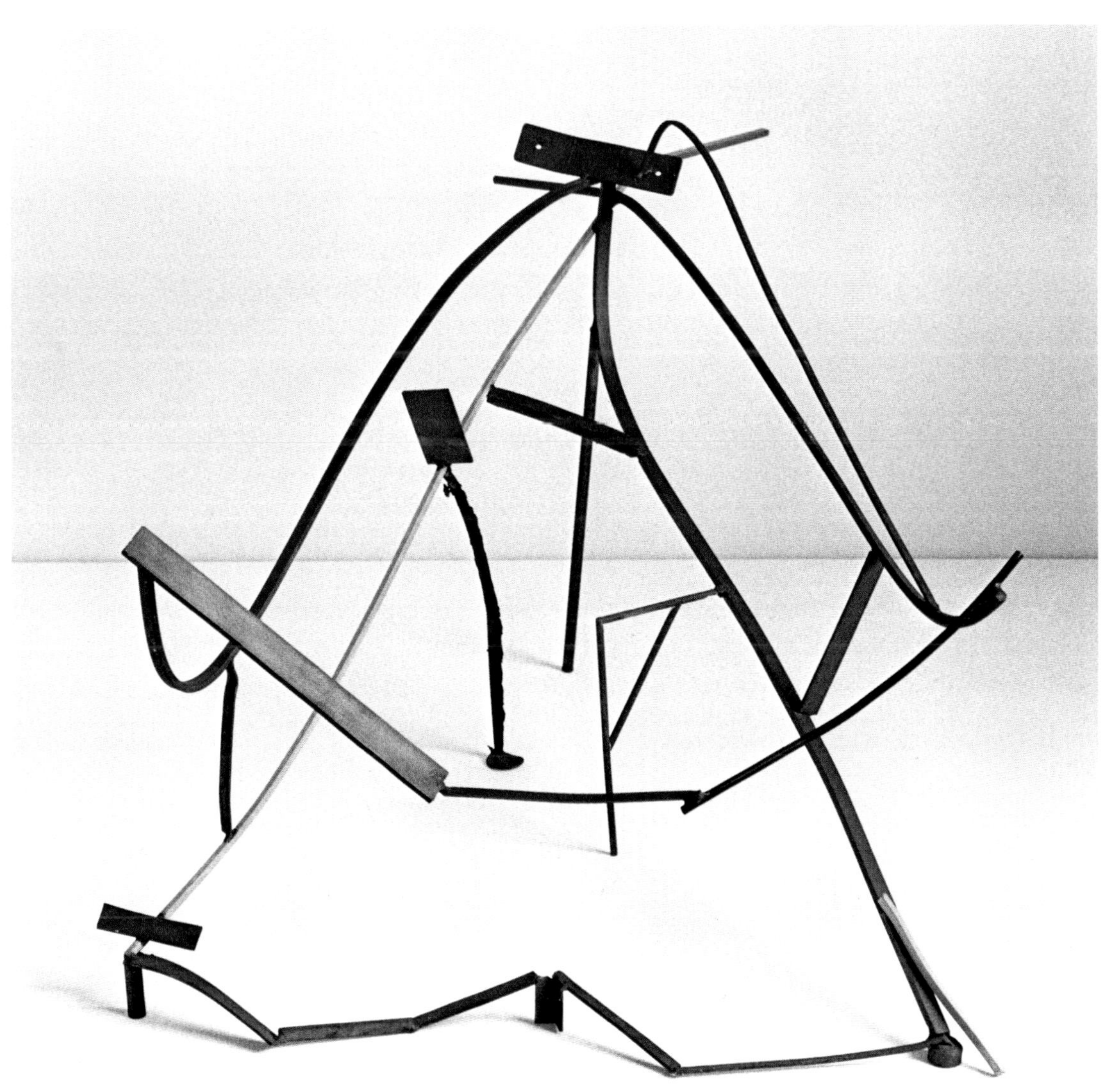

Jiminey, 1982
23 x 45 x 27 inches
Brass
Courtesy Andre
Emmerich Gallery,
New York

EXHIBITION CHECKLIST

1. Willem de Kooning
   Untitled XIII, 1969
   15¼ x 12¼ x 4½ inches
   Bronze
   David T. Owsley Collection

2. Willem de Kooning
   Floating Figure, 1972
   24 x 13 x 12 inches
   Bronze
   Collection of Paul and Camille
   Oliver-Hoffman

3. Mark di Suvero
   Search for Origins, 1983
   32 x 29 x 40½ inches
   Steel
   Private Collection, New York

4. Herbert Ferber
   Semaphore Series #2, 1983
   32¼ x 22 x 22¼ inches
   Brass, copper, and painted canvas
   Herbert Ferber, Courtesy
   M. Knoedler and Co., Inc.,
   New York

5. Herbert Ferber
   Semaphore Series #5, 1983
   49 x 28 x 27 inches
   Brass, copper, and painted canvas
   Collection of Edith Ferber

6. Peter Gourfain
   Untitled, 1986
   5¾ x 2⅝ x 16 inches
   Wood and metal
   Private collection

7. Peter Gourfain
   Save the Earth, 1986
   2½ x 2½ x 30 inches
   Wood
   Courtesy of the artist and
   Patricia Hamilton, New York

8. Robert Graham
   Lise I, 1977
   67 x 10 x 6 inches
   Bronze
   Los Angeles County Museum of
   Art, purchased with Matching
   Funds of the National Endow-
   ment for the Arts and Mr. and
   Mrs. Morley Benjamin

9. Nancy Graves
   Fanning (Glass Series), 1983
   11¾ x 24½ x 17¾ inches
   Baked enamel on bronze
   Private Collection, Courtesy
   M. Knoedler and Co., Inc.,
   New York

10. Nancy Graves
    Janus (Glass Series), 1984
    20¾ x 15¼ x 10 inches
    Baked enamel on bronze
    Private Collection, Courtesy
    M. Knoedler and Co., Inc.,
    New York

11. Bryan Hunt
    King Crest, 1976
    8 x 64 x 7 inches
    Spruce wood, silk, aluminum leaf
    Solomon R. Guggenheim
    Museum, New York, Exxon
    Corporation Purchase Award

12. Bryan Hunt
    Nineteen Hundred Eighty-six,
    1980
    9 x 65 x 9 inches
    Wood, silk, paper, copper leaf
    Collection of Barbara Haskell and
    Leon Botstein, Courtesy Blum
    Helman Gallery, New York

13. Mel Kendrick
    Black Knot, 1982
    25¼ x 8 x 8¼ inches
    Poplar, painted green; base:
    black painted steel
    Storm King Art Center, Gift of
    Cynthia Hazen Polsky

14. Mel Kendrick
    Brazilian Rosewood, 1984
    23 x 10½ x 12 inches
    Oil on Brazilian rosewood
    Courtesy John Weber Gallery,
    New York

15. Mel Kendrick
    Five Piece Purple Heart,
    1982-1985
    29 x 12½ x 11 inches
    Bronze
    Collection of the artist

16. Michael McMillen
    Pequod, 1985
    16¼ x 6¾ x 19½ inches
    Wood, metal, mirror, crab claws
    Collection of the artist

17. Michael McMillen
    Titania, 1986
    51½ x 30 x 6¾ inches
    Painted wood and metal
    Collection of Henry and Maria
    Feiwel

18. Tom Otterness
Boat with Wave, 1986-1987
11½ x 11 x 9 inches
Bronze
Courtesy Brooke Alexander
Gallery, New York

19. Tom Otterness
Death, 1986-1987
9½ x 6½ x 6 inches
Bronze
Courtesy Brooke Alexander
Gallery, New York

20. Tom Otterness
Podium Figure, 1986-1987
10 x 5 x 5 inches
Bronze
Courtesy Brooke Alexander
Gallery, New York

21. Beverly Pepper
Goliath Wedge, 1978
22 x 8 x 5½ inches
Cast and forged iron
Albright-Knox Art Gallery, Gift of
Seymour H. Knox

22. Beverly Pepper
Olga's Revenge, 1981
33½ x 10½ x 10½ inches
Forged steel
Courtesy Andre Emmerich
Gallery, New York

23. Ken Price
Turk, 1983
3¼ x 3¼ x 4½ inches
Ceramic and paint
Courtesy Charles Cowles Gallery,
New York

24. Ken Price
Untitled, 1984-1987
4 x 7 x 5 inches
Fired clay with acrylic paint
Collection of Jackson Price

25. Peter Reginato
Manhattan Love Song, 1984
42 x 29 x 18 inches
Painted steel
Private collection, New York

26. Clifford Ross
Running Man, 1984
14 x 23 x 6½ inches
Wax with encaustic,
oil paint, and gilt
Collection of the artist

27. Clifford Ross
Woman in Landscape V, 1983
12¼ x 12¾ x 2 inches
Bronze with color patina
Collection of the artist

28. Lucas Samaras
*African Winged Figure With
Head On Knee*, 1980
9½ x 10½ x 7¾ inches
Patinated bronze
Courtesy Pace Gallery, New York

29. Lucas Samaras
Grand Couple, 1980
9¾ x 7 x 7¾ inches
Patinated bronze
Courtesy Pace Gallery, New York

30. Lucas Samaras
Spanish Embrace, 1980
11 x 5 x 6½ inches
Patinated bronze
Courtesy Pace Gallery, New York

31. Joel Shapiro
untitled, 1973-1974
3 x 27⅛ x 2⅜ inches
Iron and chipboard
Collection Paula Cooper,
New York

32. Joel Shapiro
untitled, 1975-1976
3½ x 21⅛ x 28¾ inches
Bronze
Collection of the artist, New York

33. Joel Shapiro
untitled, 1978
6¹¹⁄₁₆ x 23⁷⁄₁₆ x 15¾ inches
Bronze
Collection of the artist, New York

34. Charles Simonds
Kiln, circa 1972
7 x 24 x 21 inches
Unfired clay, clay powder, lumps
of charcoal and dried moss
Collection of Monique and
Foster Goldstrom

35. James Wolfe
Jiminey, 1982
23 x 45 x 27 inches
Brass
Courtesy Andre Emmerich Gallery,
New York

CREDITS

BIG little SCULPTURE Project
Phyllis Tuchman, Curator
The Studley Press, Dalton, Mass.,
Catalogue Printing
Proforma, Pittsfield, Mass.,
Pedestal Design & Fabrication
W. Rod Faulds, Exhibition/Catalogue
Design
Deborah Menaker, Project Manager
Vivian Patterson, Registrarial Support
Saundra Goldman, Bibliographies and
Biographies
Susan Dillmann, Editor
George Abbott, Gary Sojkowski, Tim
Sedlock, Exhibition Installation
Jon Sorenson, Christina Yang, Graduate
Interns

Curator's Acknowledgements
For their generous help I'm grateful to:
Douglas G. Schultz, director, Albright-Knox
Art Gallery, Buffalo; Richard Pierce, public
information director, Brooklyn Museum;
Diane Waldman, deputy director, Solomon
R. Guggenheim Museum; Stephanie Barron
and Judy Freeman, curators, Los Angeles
County Museum of Art; Mary Jane Jacob,
chief curator, Museum of Contemporary
Art, Los Angeles; David R. Collens, director,
Storm King Art Center, Mountainville;
Patterson Sims, curator, Whitney Museum
of American Art; Peter Freeman, Blum
Helman Gallery; Theodore Bonin and
Brooke Alexander, Brooke Alexander
Gallery; Mary Jo Marks and Morgan
Spangle, Leo Castelli Gallery; Jim Cohen
and Paula Cooper, Paula Cooper Gallery;
Jennifer Lee, Lindsay Walt, and Charles
Cowles, Charles Cowles Gallery; Will
Ameringer and Dorsey Waxter, Andre
Emmerich Gallery; Jill Weinberg, Xavier
Fourcade; Mary Mulcahy, Sidney Janis
Gallery; Lori Friedman and Julian
Weissman, M. Knoedler & Co.; Lynn
Sharpless, Margo Leavin Gallery, Los
Angeles; Nathan Kernan, Robert Miller
Gallery; Jeanne Blake, Oil & Steel Gallery,
Long Island City; Douglas Baxter and Peter
Boris, Pace Gallery; Heather Nevin, Salander-
O'Reilly Galleries, Inc.; Elyse Goldberg,
Joyce Nereux, and John Weber, John
Weber Gallery; Ann Cook, Willard Gallery;
Deborah Beblo; Janet Goleas; Jay Gorney;
Patricia Hamilton; and Edvard Lieber.

Thanks also to collectors Ruth Bowman,
Mr. and Mrs. Henry Feiwel, Leonore S. and
Bernard A. Greenberg, Monique and Foster
Goldstrom, Agnes Gund, Barbara Haskell
and Leon Botstein, Camille and Paul Oliver-
Hoffman, and David T. Owsley. I've
appreciated as well the assistance of many
of the artists in the exhibition. And special
thanks to Lib Stone and Magoo and Kevin
Drewyer, Class of 1982, Williams College.

Williams College Museum of Art
Thomas Krens, Director
W. Rod Faulds, Assistant Director
Nancy M. Mathews, Prendergast Curator
Gwendolyn Owens, Prendergast Fellow
Vivian Patterson, Associate Curator,
Collections Management
Deborah Menaker, Associate Curator,
Exhibitions
Michael Govan, Special Projects
Joseph Thompson, Special Projects
Patricia Leach, Education Program Director
Zelda Stern, Public Relations Director
Elizabeth Miller, Registrar
George Abbott, Preparator
Judith M. Raab, Assistant to the Director
Pamela Ivinski, Project Assistant,
Prendergast Systematic Catalogue Project
Sally Shafto, Special Assistant to the
Director
Hanne Booth, Executive Secretary
Linda Bartlett, Accounting Secretary
Ricki Sokol, Secretary
Amber Chand, Museum Shop Manager
Saundra Goldman, NEA Intern
Graduate Interns:
Sophia Gellar, Marion Goethals, Jeanine
Gordon, Jennifer Huffman, Marni Kessler,
Yumi Nakayama, Nora Nirk, Margaret
O'Brien, Kathryn Potts, Paul Provost, Jon
Sorenson, Christina Yang, Ellen Zieselman
Security Officers:
Lawrence James Murphy, Mario Trenti,
William A. Steuer, Kenneth Gamache,
Alan Bagley

WCMA Visting Committee
Nicholas H. Wright, Chairman
Felicia Aaron, Merrill C. Berman, Robert T.
Buck, Jr., Mary Spivy Dangremond,
Maxwell Davison III, James S. Deely,
Michael S. Engl, S. Lane Faison, James
Rathbone Falck, Wendy Farrell, Liza
Fosburgh, Allan W. Fulkerson, George W.
George, Bernard Heineman, Jr., Norman
Hirschl, William Hutton, Leslie B. Keno,
Stephen F. Kiechel, Mary Lou Kroh, John
R. Lane, Jacques E. Lennon, Judith Weiss
Levy, Roger Mandel, William O'Reilly,
Stephen D. Paine, Earl A. Powell III,
Mrs. Charles Prendergast, Tennyson
Schad, Stephen F. Selig, Martin Shubik,
Whitney S. Stoddard, Suzi Stone, James
N. Wood, Martha Wright
Advisory Members: David S. Brooke,
Samuel Y. Edgerton, Jr., Gerald R. Hoepfner,
Kathleen McNally-Wassenar, Robert L. Volz
Ex-Officio Members: Francis C. Oakley, Ed
Epping, Thomas Krens
Committee Coordinator: Judith M. Raab